NEW HAVEN FREE PUBLIC LIBRARY
3 5000 09593
W9-DIY-186

Eating Disorders

Other Books of Related Interest:

At Issue Series

Alcohol Abuse

Can Diets Be Harmful?

Global Viewpoints Series

Obesity

Introducing Issues with Opposing Viewpoints Series

Drug Abuse

Issues That Concern You Series

Risky Teen Behavior

Opposing Viewpoints Series

Eating Disorders

Nutrition

Eating Disorders

Margaret Haerens

GREENHAVEN PRESS
A part of Gale, Cengage Learning

Detroit • New York • San Francisco • New Haven, Conn • Waterville, Maine • London

Elizabeth Des Chenes, *Director, Publishing Solutions*

For more information, contact:
Greenhaven Press
27500 Drake Rd.
Farmington Hills, MI 48331-3535
Or you can visit our Internet site at gale.cengage.com

LIBRARY OF CONGRESS CATALOGING-IN-PUBLICATION DATA

Eating disorders / Margaret Haerens, book editor.
p. cm. -- (Global viewpoints)
Includes bibliographical references and index.
ISBN 978-0-7377-6263-1 (hardback) -- ISBN 978-0-7377-6439-0 (paperback)
1. Eating disorders--Juvenile literature. 2. Eating disorders--Social aspects--Juvenile literature. I. Haerens, Margaret.
RC552.E18E2814 2012
616.85'26--dc23

2012009508

Printed in Mexico
2 3 4 5 6 7 16 15 14 13 12

Contents

Foreword 13

Introduction 16

Chapter 1: Eating Disorder Trends

1. Eating Disorders Are a Global Problem 22

Something Fishy

For years it was thought that eating disorders affected only young, white middle- and upper-class women from Western countries. That assumption has been proven false, as eating disorders have spread across class, race, ethnicity, and religion. Eating disorders have also spread across the globe and have become a worldwide problem, showing up in countries such as Japan, Argentina, and China.

2. Western Celebrities Are Particularly Susceptible to Orthorexia 28

Judith Woods

Orthorexia is characterized by an obsession with the quality of food one consumes. Orthorexics become so focused on eating organic, vegan, or healthy foods that they strictly limit their diets and often deprive their bodies of much-needed nutrients. Celebrities are prone to orthorexia because they feel pressure to maintain a thin body image; by focusing only on healthy foods, celebrities appear to be disciplined and in good physical shape.

3. The **United States** Recognizes the Recent Trend of Drunkorexia 35

Ashley Jennings

The American media have reported on a new trend in eating disorders known as drunkorexia. Men and women who suffer from the condition restrict their food intake in order to indulge in binge eating and drinking alcohol. Studies have shown that people are more susceptible to drunkorexia in college, when many men and women begin to develop unhealthy relationships with food and alcohol.

Chapter 4: Strategies to Curb Eating Disorders

Studies have shown that the rates of eating disorders in Asian and Western countries are comparable. In Malaysia, there has been no comprehensive study to determine how prevalent eating disorders are, although experts assert that they are on the rise. Malaysians struggling with eating disorders are usually referred to Singapore for treatment because Malaysia does not have the proper facilities or treatment resources for victims.

9. The **Philippines** Is Ignoring the Problem of Eating Disorders **195**

Natasha B. Gamalinda

It is troubling that there aren't any statistics regarding eating disorders in the Philippines. It reveals the nation's attitudes about eating disorders; the government and health establishment ignore eating disorders and families are in denial until the victims are almost beyond help. Attitudes must change, and the country must come to terms with and address the growing problem of eating disorders.

Periodical and Internet Sources Bibliography **202**

For Further Discussion **203**

Organizations to Contact **205**

Bibliography of Books **211**

Index **214**

Foreword

> *"The problems of all of humanity can only be solved by all of humanity."*
> *—Swiss author Friedrich Dürrenmatt*

Global interdependence has become an undeniable reality. Mass media and technology have increased worldwide access to information and created a society of global citizens. Understanding and navigating this global community is a challenge, requiring a high degree of information literacy and a new level of learning sophistication.

Building on the success of its flagship series, Opposing Viewpoints, Greenhaven Press has created the Global Viewpoints series to examine a broad range of current, often controversial topics of worldwide importance from a variety of international perspectives. Providing students and other readers with the information they need to explore global connections and think critically about worldwide implications, each Global Viewpoints volume offers a panoramic view of a topic of widespread significance.

Drugs, famine, immigration—a broad, international treatment is essential to do justice to social, environmental, health, and political issues such as these. Junior high, high school, and early college students, as well as general readers, can all use Global Viewpoints anthologies to discern the complexities relating to each issue. Readers will be able to examine unique national perspectives while, at the same time, appreciating the interconnectedness that global priorities bring to all nations and cultures.

Material in each volume is selected from a diverse range of sources, including journals, magazines, newspapers, nonfiction books, speeches, government documents, pamphlets, organization newsletters, and position papers. Global Viewpoints is truly global, with material drawn primarily from international sources available in English and secondarily from US sources with extensive international coverage.

Features of each volume in the Global Viewpoints series include:

- An **annotated table of contents** that provides a brief summary of each essay in the volume, including the name of the country or area covered in the essay.
- An **introduction** specific to the volume topic.
- A **world map** to help readers locate the countries or areas covered in the essays.
- For each viewpoint, an **introduction** that contains notes about the author and source of the viewpoint explains why material from the specific country is being presented, summarizes the main points of the viewpoint, and offers three **guided reading questions** to aid in understanding and comprehension.
- **For further discussion** questions that promote critical thinking by asking the reader to compare and contrast aspects of the viewpoints or draw conclusions about perspectives and arguments.
- A worldwide list of **organizations to contact** for readers seeking additional information.
- A **periodical bibliography** for each chapter and a **bibliography of books** on the volume topic to aid in further research.
- A comprehensive **subject index** to offer access to people, places, events, and subjects cited in the text, with the countries covered in the viewpoints highlighted.

Global Viewpoints is designed for a broad spectrum of readers who want to learn more about current events, history, political science, government, international relations, economics, environmental science, world cultures, and sociology—students doing research for class assignments or debates, teachers and faculty seeking to supplement course materials, and others wanting to understand current issues better. By presenting how people in various countries perceive the root causes, current consequences, and proposed solutions to worldwide challenges, Global Viewpoints volumes offer readers opportunities to enhance their global awareness and their knowledge of cultures worldwide.

Introduction

> *"For some, dieting, bingeing, and purging may begin as a way to cope with painful emotions and to feel in control of one's life, but ultimately, these behaviors will damage a person's physical and emotional health, self-esteem, and sense of competence and control."*
>
> *—National Eating Disorders Association*

Eating disorders are not recent phenomenas. There is evidence that anorexia nervosa and bulimia have been around for centuries; in some cases, these conditions have been condoned and encouraged by medical, political, sociocultural, and religious authorities. Throughout history, anorexia nervosa and bulimia were not always recognized as deadly health risks. If they were, physicians and families often did not have a way to effectively treat them. It was not until the twentieth century when eating disorders were finally understood as psychological disorders tied to distorted body images that a method of treatment was implemented that took into account physical, mental, and emotional factors.

However, the twentieth century also brought new technologies and media that promoted unhealthy body images and disseminated information about eating disorders across the globe. With the rise of television, movies, and the Internet, men and women were able to compare their bodies to those of stick-thin fashion models and celebrities and embark on strictly observed diets or a pattern of bingeing and purging that could evolve into full-blown eating disorders. By the dawn of the twenty-first century, eating disorders had become a global problem that affected young and old, men and women, and developing and developed countries.

There are numerous historical references to the practice of bingeing and purging in antiquity. Ancient Egyptian physicians prescribed purgation, or the process of making oneself vomit, not to lose weight but because of the widespread belief that some foods caused disease. In ancient Rome, men and women binged on foods and then purged to make room for other courses or to try other dishes. Many historians believe that Romans tickled the back of their throats with feathers in order to purge large meals—but then went back to the table to continue the feast. It is believed that in many cultures throughout history, it was commonplace to binge when food was available and then purge to make room for more food. The Talmud, an ancient Hebrew text, had a name for such a pattern: *boolmot*, a ravenous hunger that should be treated with sweet foods. According to the Talmud, if an individual was "seized with bulimy" on Yom Kippur, they must be fed unclean things. Throughout the Middle Ages, purgation remained a recommended remedy for a number of physical conditions and was culturally accepted.

Anorexia nervosa can be traced back to the Middle Ages. Instead of starving themselves to be thin, women fasted in order to be closer to God; this practice became known as anorexia mirabilis. During the era, there were many accounts of young Christian women starving themselves for days on end, often in conjunction with other ascetic practices like chastity, self-flagellation, and sleeping on a bed of thorns. These women, called "miracle maidens," were highly venerated; it was thought that their self-discipline and sacrifice proved that they were touched by God. Many of these young, devoted women and girls starved themselves to death. One prominent example of this trend was Saint Catherine of Siena (1347–1380), an Italian woman who believed that eating was capitulation to temptation and that by extreme fasting she was proving her complete devotion to God. For Saint Catherine and other young women, anorexia was a way to attract approval and admiration as a pious, exceptional Christian and assert their independence and female identity.

In 1869 an English physician, Richard Morton, published a landmark paper that offered a medical description of anorexia nervosa. "Phtisiologia: A Treatise on Consumption" describes a "wasting" disease of nervous origins that involves patients refusing to eat to the point of severe emaciation and even death. In 1873 another English physician, Sir William Gull, published his "Anorexia Nervosa," a paper that describes three cases of anorexia and clearly defines it as a psychological disorder.

In the twentieth century, psychiatrists, scientists, and physicians worked to find the causes for eating disorders, develop accurate diagnostic techniques, and put in place effective treatment programs for bulimia and anorexia nervosa. In 1973 a German-born psychoanalyst named Hilde Bruch published *Eating Disorders: Obesity, Anorexia Nervosa, and the Person Within*, a landmark study that posited that bulimic and anorexic patients suffered from distorted body images.

In the 1970s and 1980s, eating disorders were recognized as an epidemic in Western countries. Anorexia and bulimia garnered reputations for being "a rich girl's disease," because they overwhelmingly affected young, privileged white girls. By the turn of the century, however, it was clear that eating disorders had spread from the West to other cultures and regions, especially Japan, China, Russia, and parts of South America. What was once alleged to be a disease that struck only rich white girls in Western countries was spreading across the globe and economic and cultural barriers.

The authors of the viewpoints presented in *Global Viewpoints: Eating Disorders* discuss some of the key issues of worldwide concern: the spread of eating disorders to developing nations; the role of media in perceptions of body image; the connection among body image, religious and cultural expectations, and eating disorders; and strategies to prevent and treat such conditions. The information in this volume provides insight into the challenges that many countries face in confronting these disorders and providing effective treatment for men and women suffering from eating disorders. It also offers information on emerging trends in the field and the increasing prevalence of eating disorders among men and older women.

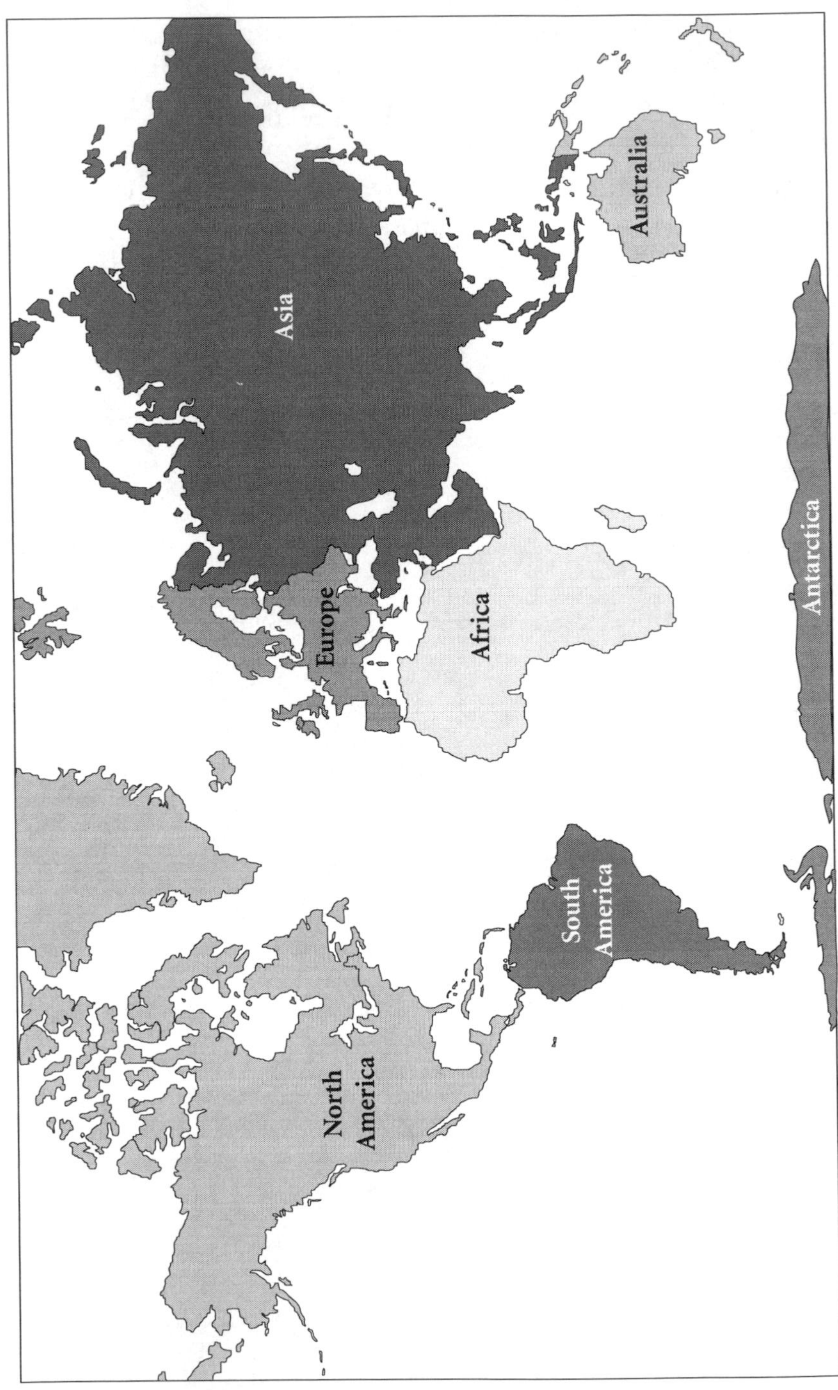
Asia
Australia
Europe
Africa
Antarctica
North America
South America

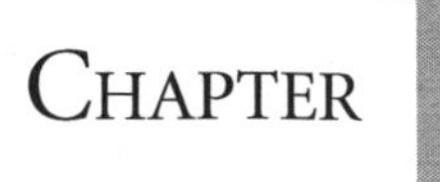

Eating Disorder Trends

VIEWPOINT 1

Eating Disorders Are a Global Problem

Something Fishy

Something Fishy is a website that features a wide range of information on eating disorders. In the following viewpoint, the author maintains that eating disorders, once thought to afflict only white upper- or middle-class American women, are found in every stratum of women in the United States. In fact, they are found all over the world and are particularly prevalent in Japan and Argentina. Eating disorders can be found all over the world, according to Something Fishy, because the pressures and motivations associated with these conditions are universal.

As you read, consider the following questions:

1. What two celebrities does the author identify as having body images that young Hispanic and African American women may try to emulate?
2. Why does the author say that it is nearly impossible to determine exactly how many victims of eating disorders are in Japan?
3. According to Lori Leibovich, why do some people blame Argentina's machismo culture for the country's high rates of eating disorders?

"Cultural Roles," Something Fishy, Website on Eating Disorders, 2007. www.something-fishy.org.

It was once a widely held belief that the only people who suffered from eating disorders were white, middle- to upper-class American women. I can tell you, from the hundreds to thousands of e-mail letters I have received from the sufferers themselves, by far, white women are not the only ones suffering.

A great number of researchers are focusing in on why there seems to be an increase in the growing number of black, Hispanic, Asian and Native American sufferers who are coming forward to say that they indeed are afflicted with an eating disorder.

As African-American and Hispanic women compete more and more in the professional job market . . . they can be faced with discrimination as well as society's portrayal of the successful "smart, beautiful and thin" career woman.

The Prevalence of Eating Disorders

[*Essence Magazine*] featured an article on the subject of eating disorders in black women, providing a possible insight. "The Black-American culture traditionally accepts more fat on women than the White culture, but when Black middle-class women become integrated into White culture while they are trying to get ahead, they become more at risk of developing eating disorders."

As African-American and Hispanic women compete more and more in the professional job market and face the pressures of trying to succeed, they can be faced with discrimination as well as society's portrayal of the successful "smart, beautiful and thin" career woman.

There has been a steady increase in famous African-American and Hispanic figures in the media. While this is a wonderful thing that helps to represent the truly diverse country the United States is, there may also be a "downside" as

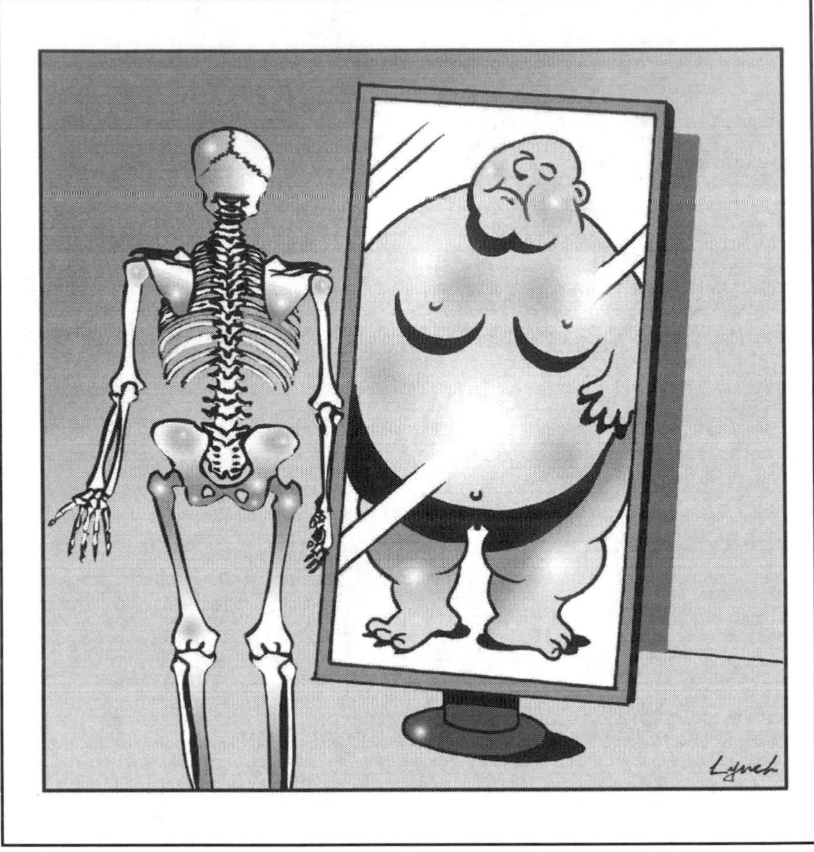

"What disorder," cartoon by Mark Lynch, www.CartoonStock.com. Copyright © Mark Lynch. Reproduction rights obtainable from www.CartoonStock.com.

well. Young white women and girls faced with thin and beautiful white celebrities aspire to be like them—it would make sense to think that young black and Hispanic women and girls, when faced with seemingly beautiful and thin celebrities sharing the same culture (such as Janet Jackson or Mariah Carey), might also wish to achieve the same physical goals.

Body Image and Eating Disorders

The psychological reasons that women of color develop eating disorders are virtually the same: family problems, parents with negative coping mechanisms like alcohol, history of abuse, and/or relationship issues, plus a need to cope with stress, pain and anger, and a low self-esteem. In addition, black, Asian, Hispanic and Native American women also face issues of discrimination that may contribute to their low self-worth and desire to be loved and accepted.

From the About-Face organization's website: "The more a person is pressured to emulate the mainstream image, the more the desire to be thin is adopted, and with it an increased risk for the development of body image dissatisfaction and eating disorders."

It is important to take into consideration the awareness that has spread in the last fifteen or so years about eating disorders themselves. Whereas issues of culture may not be addressed often enough, there may still be a better overall knowledge of what these disorders are, throughout a more diverse community. Whether teens and college students are getting the education at their school, through clinics and women's centers, through the television or on the Internet, *all groups of people* may be more apt to recognize that they are suffering from an illness and are not alone. Prior to 1980, it was highly unlikely that any information, let alone accurate information, was reaching anyone other than through doctors' offices typically treating the white, middle-to-upper-class community. It is highly possible that until recently, due to lack of awareness and the stereotype that this was a "white teen or college woman's disease," many women of color were either suffering in silence or didn't recognize how severe their problem could be.

It's a Small World

Eating disorders are one of the most common psychological problems facing young women in Tokyo, Japan. According to a Japanese certified clinical psychologist, many who came for counseling often gave their reason for doing so as experiencing problems in having healthy interpersonal relationships

The Prevalence of Eating Disorders

Eating disorders are pervasive, affecting up to 24 million Americans and 70 million individuals worldwide. Once thought of as diseases of upper-middle-class adolescents, recent research has shown that eating disorders cross racial, religious, ethnic, and socioeconomic lines and that 10–15% of those suffering with eating disorders are men.

Susan Blumenthal and Beth Hoffman, "Eating Disorders Awareness Week," Huffington Post, *February 23, 2010. www.huffingtonpost.com.*

such as with family or in social environments such as at college or within the workplace. There is still a great shame attached to seeking counseling in Japan, and for this, many people do not get the help they need or deserve. It also makes it nearly impossible to determine exactly how many victims of eating disorders are in Japan.

In Argentina the incidence rate of anorexia and bulimia is out of control. The percentage of sufferers (based on population) is almost three times greater than that of the United States. Women across Argentina will resort, at all costs, to look their best and are obsessed with their bodies. According to an article written by Lori Leibovich, "Some blamed the nation's preoccupation with the body on the country's volatile political and economic climate. Others said that the Italian immigrants who settled in Argentina at the turn of the century simply brought with them a flair for fashion and an appreciation of beauty. And some Argentine feminists say that 'machismo' is responsible for the epidemic, encouraging a climate where women are valued for how they look, not who they are." Women that don't fit the harsh Argentine ideal end up in their own world of self-hate.

Eating disorders are on the rise in China and experts feel this may have to do with the rise of diet fads throughout that region. Advertising of diet products that flood the market emphasize to the public that life is better when a person is slim, so sufferers faced with problems in their life may turn to dieting as an answer. Not to say that all people who diet will end up struggling with an eating disorder, but persons with a low self-esteem who may have been susceptible to workaholism, alcoholism or drug addiction, will now also be more at risk for developing an eating disorder.

No Discrimination

Either way, no matter what color, race, cultural background or sexual orientation a sufferer comes from, the eating disorders that affect them are devastating. Each person, male or female, is suffering inside from the emotional turmoil that led them to seek comfort from anorexia, bulimia or compulsive overeating. . . . And like I have said hundreds of times, each of them deserves to find help and recovery so that they may learn to love themselves, inside and out.

Viewpoint 2

Western Celebrities Are Particularly Susceptible to Orthorexia

Judith Woods

Judith Woods is a features writer for the Telegraph. *In the following viewpoint, she introduces the eating disorder orthorexia nervosa, which involves a discerning preoccupation with the purity of food. Woods classifies orthorexia as a growing disorder, especially among Western celebrities. Because most celebrities are obsessed with staying thin, Woods asserts, they are particularly prone to developing this disorder. Orthorexia allows men and women to limit their diets severely and then brag that they eat only healthy food. In reality, Woods points out, they have developed orthorexia nervosa and may be depriving themselves of much-needed nutrients.*

As you read, consider the following questions:

1. According to the author, what has British actress Sadie Frost announced about her eating habits?
2. When does the author say that the term "orthorexic" was first used?
3. Why does Deanne Jade believe that orthorexia is "very much a disease of the 21st century"?

Judith Woods, "Orthorexia: Dirty Secrets of the Health-Food Junkies," *The Telegraph*, February 22, 2008. www.telegraph.co.uk.

Dinner out with old friends. How relaxing to catch up over food—at least that was the theory. In practice, I found myself trapped in the Seventh Circle of macrobiotic, non-GM [genetically modified], low-sodium Hell. Friend number one, it transpires, has an allergy to wheat and dairy (middle-class euphemism for "I'm on a diet").

Friend number two apparently eats only superfoods, but it's very hard to find a decent restaurant that serves nothing but goji berries.

Friend three is entirely additive free, and friends four and five are the sort of born-again organic evangelists who take turns to interrogate the waiter, as though he were some kind of hostile witness deliberately trying to conceal the exact provenance of the sea salt.

I was made to feel a complete pleb [a plebeian, or commoner] because I didn't go off-menu, ate everything I ordered and enjoyed it with what my companions felt was peasant-like gusto.

A Food Minefield

I was reminded of my pernickety social circle when Sadie Frost [a British actress] announced this week [in February 2008] that she has a horror of eating what she called "dirty" food. At first I assumed she meant she was too precious to scoop spilled pasta out of the sink and pop it back in the saucepan.

But no, by "dirty" she meant food that wasn't organic. I think I actually screamed aloud in outrage as I read her princess words.

Just when did we all get so hung up about food? As the arguments over food labelling rumble on, and the government even considers paying fat people to lose weight, our society has become polarised as never before.

At one end of the spectrum we have rampant obesity, with whole sections of the population gorging themselves to an early grave. On the other, we have anorexics, starving themselves below size zero.

What Are Orthorexics?

And then we have the orthorexics, a growing section of society whose fastidious preoccupation with the purity of their food has led to them being given their own eating disorder category: orthorexia nervosa.

"For orthorexics, a fixation with what they eat becomes an all-consuming lifestyle," says Dr Alex Yellowlees, medical director of the Priory Hospital in Glasgow [Scotland].

Other eating disorders focus on quantity of food, but orthorexics are solely concerned with its quality.

"They are so concerned with foods that are 'good' and foods that are 'bad' that their diet suffers, their personal relationships come under pressure and they end up socially isolated, because the simple act of eating has become so stressful."

The term "orthorexic" comes from the Greek ortho, meaning straight and correct, and was first coined in 1996 by Dr Steven Bratman, the American author of *Health Food Junkies: Orthorexia Nervosa*.

Other eating disorders focus on quantity of food, but orthorexics are solely concerned with its quality. They obsess over salt content and E numbers [codes for food additives], refuse to eat sugar and fat, and have such a hang-up about healthy eating that it restricts their diet and can, paradoxically, make them undernourished.

"We're certainly seeing more of this behaviour," says Dr Yellowlees. "Like other eating disorders, the issue at the heart of it all is obsession. Part of it has to do with the way we're constantly bombarded with media messages about what's healthy and what isn't. People don't quite know what to believe, so they lose a sense of perspective.

"They also take a certain enjoyment from refusing food in front of others, as a way of demonstrating their superior commitment to the purity of what they eat."

A Rising Condition

Although there are, as yet, no figures available for the number of orthorexia sufferers, anecdotal evidence suggests that equal numbers of men and women are affected. The growth of our complementary therapy culture is a key factor in the spread of orthorexia.

As we look beyond conventional medicine to keep us healthy, diet becomes more important—whether that involves cutting out foods that we believe harm us or placing great emphasis on foods that will heal us. Parents who mistakenly believe that all fat is bad, for example, will cause malnutrition in their children by removing it from their diets.

The growth of our complementary therapy culture is a key factor in the spread of orthorexia.

Orthorexia and Celebrities

Celebrities are particularly prone to orthorexia. In the world of show business, where body image is so important, it's no surprise to learn that Victoria Beckham breakfasts on algae and seaweed shakes and snacks on edamame beans or that Gwyneth Paltrow religiously adheres to a macrobiotic diet.

Natalie Portman and Uma Thurman mostly eat raw food and, perhaps most bizarrely of all, Reese Witherspoon tucks into jars of organic baby food, which she carries around in her handbag.

The Serious Nature of Orthorexia

Generally, orthorexia can be considered when the eating disorder is long term and not transitory, and when such behaviour has a significant negative impact on the quality of life of the individual. Orthorexic subjects, in extreme cases, will prefer to starve themselves rather than eat foods which they consider "impure" and thus harmful to their health.

In view of these considerations, orthorexia could be considered to be a more or less serious personality or behavioural disturbance which has very little to do with trends or behaviour linked to religious or philosophical customs.

L.M. Donini, D. Marsili, M.P. Graziani, M. Imbriale, and C. Cannella, "Orthorexia Nervosa: A Preliminary Study with a Proposal for Diagnosis and an Attempt to Measure the Dimension of the Phenomenon," Eating and Weight Disorders, *June 2004.*

The Reality of Orthorexia

So far, so La-La Land. But it seems the rest of us—my friends included—are catching up fast. Anna Brook, 41, from London, only eats organic food, avoids gluten, wheat and dairy and admits she spends hours a day thinking about sourcing and preparing her next meal.

She brings her own box of salad to work every day, so she can be sure of exactly what she will be eating, and she rarely accepts dinner invitations because she gets stressed about what might be served.

"Food rules my life. I don't think I've drunk tap water for five years, and I only ever cook with filtered water," she says. "I have cupboards stacked with virtuous herbal teas that I drink but don't actually like and I will beat myself up for days if I weaken and eat biscuits or crisps, because I will imagine how my system is being poisoned."

Is her attitude the self-indulgence of a card-carrying member of the worried well—or a reflection of a deeper malaise in our overanxious society?

The Power of Food Industry Marketeers

According to Michael Pollan, the American author of *In Defense of Food*, a newly published rallying cry to return to a balanced diet, we've been bamboozled and frightened en masse by the food industry marketeers.

"We are all suffering from the effects of the pseudo-biochemistry that's peddled by food manufacturers," says Pollan.

"Nobody really knows what an antioxidant does, but we're sold this line that they are good for us, so instead of eating wholesome normal food, we spend our money on processed stuff that isn't nearly as good for us.

"There's no evidence that worrying about your nutritional health improves it, even though more and more of us are doing it. We all need to get back to eating fresh, nutritious food. For me that corresponds to 'Don't eat anything your great-grandmother wouldn't recognise as food.'"

The Narcissism of Orthorexia

Fine sentiments, but whereas 20 years ago so-called health-food freaks were marginalised, orthorexics today are a vocal bunch who opine openly about their faddy food convictions—and who strive to gain social kudos for their culinary asceticism.

"Orthorexics feel special and different because of their eating habits," says Deanne Jade, founder of the National Centre for Eating Disorders. "It's often a behaviour adopted by people without any strong sense of self.

"They want to be noticed and to impress others by talking knowledgeably about food. It's all very narcissistic and is quite irritating to be around.

"Like any eating disorder, there are degrees to which people are affected, but this is becoming a widespread phenomenon. These days we're all encouraged to do a lot of navel-gazing and self-analysis, and orthorexia is very much a disease of the 21st century."

Tough Love

And what begins as an affectation can, in some cases, undoubtedly progress to an illness. So perhaps it's up to the rest of us to stand firm at the outset and deprive faddy eaters of all that attention before it escalates out of control.

So next time I'm seeing friends, I shall take the tough love option. I'll invite them to dinner and tell them it's my treat. Then I'll arrive half an hour early—and order for everyone.

Viewpoint 3

The United States Recognizes the Recent Trend of Drunkorexia

Ashley Jennings

Ashley Jennings is a member of the ABC News on Campus bureau. In the following viewpoint, she reports on the emerging trend of drunkorexia, a condition in which young men and women restrict their caloric intake in order to use them for binge drinking. While women do it to control their weight, Jennings says, some men practice drunkorexia for financial reasons—eliminating food means more money for beer. Jennings discusses drunkorexia as a disease that has its roots in addiction and is often linked with alcoholism.

As you read, consider the following questions:

1. According to a study by the University of Texas School of Public Health and the University of North Texas Health Science Center, what is the trend of binge drinking?
2. How many females suffer from some sort of eating disorder, according to the National Eating Disorders Association?

Ashley Jennings, "Drunkorexia: Alcohol Mixes with Eating Disorders," ABCNews.com, October 21, 2010. abcnews.go.com.

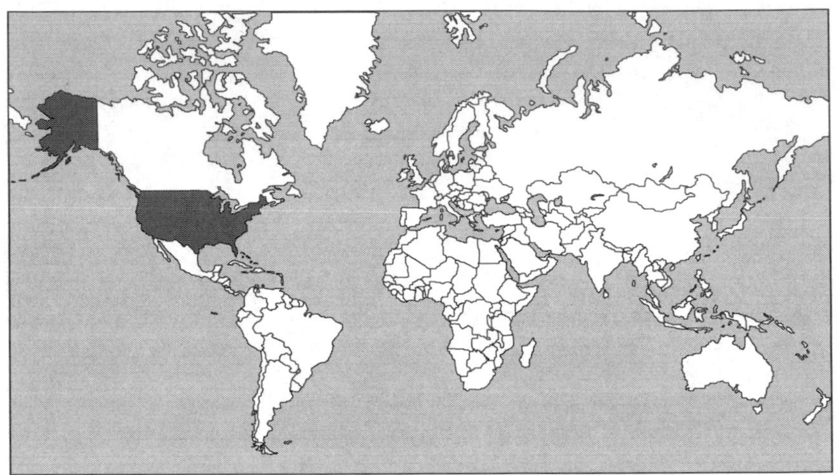

3. How many men suffer from some sort of eating disorder, according to the National Eating Disorders Association?

As college campuses participate in Fat-Talk Free Week—a national campaign to raise awareness of the perils of conversation that regularly includes "I'm so fat" and "You look great! Have you lost weight?"—anorexia and bulimia aren't the only eating disorders on the table.

Over the past few years a new dietary trend has popped up on celebrity chatters and websites and in newspaper articles. The *New York Times* and Jezebel.com have covered it, and just this week *Denver Post* columnist Kristen Browning-Blas reported on it in an article that's being widely reprinted.

The trend is "drunkorexia."

What Is Drunkorexia?

"Abuse counselors are putting the word 'drunkorexia' in line with other eating disorders because the patient uses the same type of methods as anorexia and bulimia—they just mix it with alcohol too," said Dr. Kevin Prince, alcohol and other drug education program coordinator at University Health Services in Austin Texas.

Diet blogs and studies describe a drunkorexic as someone who restricts food intake to reserve those calories for alcohol and binge drinking, and note that people are more susceptible to drunkorexia in college. A recent study by the University of Texas School of Public Health and the University of North Texas Health Science Center found that in the past 10 years binge drinking has increased among young men and women.

With fall semester in full swing, universities nationwide are striving to crack down on the behavior. The University of Minnesota is displaying "anti-binge drinking" ads across campus, while administrators at New York University are strictly enforcing "no drinking" dormitory rules more than ever.

They have a tough fight ahead.

Savannah, a 22-year-old University of Texas [UT] graduate from Houston, agreed to be interviewed by ABCNews.com as long as her last name was not used.

An alumna of the Greek community, Savannah says it was easy to abstain from food when it came time to party, with the help of a support system made up of friends and sorority sisters.

"I've always watched my weight and skipped meals to account for the high calorie count of alcohol," said Savannah. "It was just something I always did while in college as a normal part of my diet so that I could stay skinny but still go out and drink."

Trading Tips

Savannah says she and her friends would trade methods for skipping meals: working out late at night instead of eating, having one medium meal during the day, in some cases throwing up before going out.

Even though the group knew it was wrong, it became part of the young women's weekend routine.

"I do know a lot of people who skip meals to drink, drink heavily, and don't gain any weight. Obviously their success in this way encourages others to try it," Savannah said.

During her four years in college, Savannah attended counseling sessions for anorexia, at her mother's suggestion. (According to the National Eating Disorders Association, as many as 10 million females suffer from some sort of eating disorder. Of those 10 million, 40 percent of newly identified cases of anorexia are in young women.)

"I've done [drunkorexia] for years and I'm still healthy. And I'm skinny," she said. "That's the best of both worlds to me, so it's not likely that I'll stop doing it any time soon."

Men Consider the Finance Factor

The National Eating Disorders Association shows that while women are more commonly affected by eating disorders, more than a million men and boys battle the illness every day. Between fraternity binge drinking and the social norms of alcohol on campus, college males also try to control their weight while having a good time.

Rodney, a 20-year-old public relations major at UT who also agreed to an interview under the terms that his identity be kept secret, says drunkorexia in men starts with optimizing intoxication levels.

"When you consume on an empty stomach, you feel the effect quicker," Rodney said. Last semester, "during the day on Friday I only ate a pint of ice cream all day, knowing I'd be drinking liquor later that night."

Rodney says it's also a money factor for men. If it comes between eating dinner or spending it on beer, it's often easier to go the beer route.

"Alcohol advertisements have definitely made an impact, considering you see more and more commercials associated with low-cost and low-cal beers, or what I call 'diet beers.'"

Drinking and Eating Disorders

Studies show that binge drinking and alcohol abuse are on the rise among women, who are also more prone than men to eating disorders.

About 25 to 33 percent of bulimics also struggle with alcohol or drugs, according to a study published last year [2007] in the journal *Biological Psychiatry*. Between 20 and 25 percent of anorexics have substance abuse problems, the study found.

Sarah Kershaw,
"Starving Themselves, Cocktail in Hand,"
New York Times, *March 2, 2008.*

Some students believe it is these sorts of advertisements that push peers to try drunkorexia and other drastic measures in order to stay thin.

Women as Targets

"On Facebook when we put our gender as female, we're not only targeted with bridal ads but how-to-lose-weight ads, diet ads," said Micaela Neumann, a 19-year-old communications student at UT. "Men don't get that. We are targeted to lose weight."

Advertisements aren't alone in supporting weight loss. Pro-anorexia blogs have been popping up over the past few years and are becoming popular internationally. Most websites focus on a "pro-ana" approach, which promotes the eating disorder anorexia nervosa as a lifestyle choice. Ana is a sort of mascot, the personification of an anorexic girl.

Pro-thinspo.com gives strategies for staying thin and how to "look like a model." Trends range from the "5 bite diet," in which a person only eats five bites of food every meal to stay skinny, to different detox methods. On some sites, each week there's a new technique for drinking and not gaining weight or using other forms of drugs.

"It's scary to think that there are support groups like this," said Dr. Prince.

"A lot of women I've worked with have used these drunkorexic strategies. It's a habit they've formed, and they have this mentality that you can't get your last 'hoorah' in without thinking about the consequences. Every calorie counts," Dr. Prince said.

Psychologists stress that the main cause of drunkorexia is addiction.

Along with skipping meals altogether, purging is also a danger associated with drunkorexia. A person binge drinks then binge eats (usually with foods high in salt and sugar according to Drugrehabtreatment.com) and throws it back up after.

"It's not good for you nutrition-wise, and the alcohol is going to hit your system harder because there's nothing to slow it down at first," Prince said.

Drunkorexia's Roots in Addiction

Psychologists stress that the main cause of drunkorexia is addiction.

According to the National Institute on Alcohol Abuse and Alcoholism, "alcoholism and eating disorders frequently co-occur and often co-occur in the presence of other psychiatric and personality disorders."

Because drunkorexia isn't a defined medical condition, however, doctors have to look at the conditions of these separate addictions and treat them one at a time. Prince says he works through the effects of a patient's eating disorder before counseling for alcoholism, or vice versa.

Alcoholism, Bulimia and Anorexia

Addressing the links between alcoholism, bulimia and anorexia, "where there's a great deal of overlap is in commonalities of the addiction, when there's planning and focus on engaging the addiction itself," Dr. Stewart Cooper, director of grad psychology programs and counseling services at Valparaiso University, said.

"I think it's not uncommon with chemical addictions that when one thing's not available, they'll use another," Dr. Cooper said. "They use different means to alter the experience and get away from feeling."

Ewa Kacewicz, a psychology doctoral candidate and volunteer at the center for students in recovery at the University of Texas, knows this escape from reality all too well. Prior to her volunteer work, she suffered from alcohol abuse. Based on her personal experience and the experiences of those around her, she says of drunkorexia and the blogs devoted to it, "People are taking it so lightly, as if it's some type of diet fad."

"Whether it's alcoholism, drug abuse or some type of eating disorder, an addiction is still an addiction and has to be helped," Kacewicz said. "If not, the results could be deadly."

VIEWPOINT 4

Older British Women Are Developing Anorexia

Denis Campbell

Denis Campbell is the health correspondent for the Guardian *and the* Observer. *In the following viewpoint, he reports that doctors in England are diagnosing a rising number of late-onset eating disorders, far later than the age when the conditions usually emerge. Psychiatrists are attributing this trend to a growing pressure to remain thin and attractive later in life, Campbell maintains, exacerbated by media images of older women still looking youthful and thin well into their 40s, 50s, and 60s. According to Campbell, psychiatrists find that major life events are usually the trigger, most frequently a divorce, unemployment, menopause, losing a parent, or children leaving home.*

As you read, consider the following questions:

1. How many patients a year does Dr. Sylvia Dahabra see with late-onset eating disorders?
2. According to Campbell, what is one suggestion as to why some women develop anorexia or bulimia and other women don't?
3. What mental illness has the highest mortality rate, according to the author?

Denis Campbell, "The New Anorexics: Big Increase in Eating Disorders Among Women over 30," *The Guardian*, October 8, 2010. www.guardiannews.com.

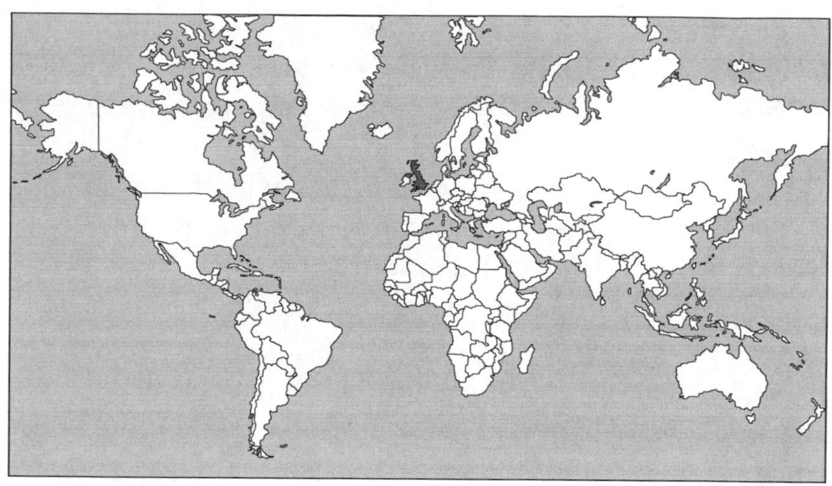

Eating disorders experts are treating growing numbers of women who are developing anorexia or bulimia well into adulthood, far beyond the teenage years when the conditions usually emerge.

Psychiatrists are seeing more patients who have become seriously ill with either of the crippling conditions for the first time in their 30s, 40s, 50s and occasionally 60s. In many cases, the illness has been triggered by a relationship breaking down, unemployment, menopause, losing a parent, or seeing children leave home.

A Troubling Trend

Some working with patients say that the rise in what are called late-onset eating disorders is linked to some women in their 40s and 50s feeling under pressure to look young because of the prominence of age-defying older female celebrities, such as Madonna and Sharon Stone.

"Five or 10 years ago, I would've seen one case of an older person developing an eating disorder about once every year or two. But now I see them more often—about five new patients a year with late-onset anorexia nervosa or bulimia," said Dr

Sylvia Dahabra, a psychiatrist in Newcastle who works for the regional specialist eating disorders service.

Sian, who didn't want to be fully identified, tells the story of her mother, Fiona, who died of anorexia in 2008 aged 48. "The trauma of me moving out of the family home at 18 to live nearby, and then relocating further away to Bournemouth when I was 21, triggered her serious decline. I was pretty much mum's life, and me leaving meant she was alone. She ended up weighing just six stone when she passed away when I was 21," said Sian. [Editor's note: There are 14 pounds in a stone.] Fiona died in her sleep after contracting bronchial pneumonia.

"Once she got the pneumonia, she couldn't fight it because her body was so weak from the anorexia," said Sian.

Triggers for Late-Onset Eating Disorders

Major life events are usually the cause of these disorders. "The person can lose their job, suffer a bereavement, have a child or see their relationship break down. As a result, their mood deteriorates and they develop a depressive illness. They lose their appetite and then lose weight," said Dahabra. "They then notice that they feel better when they don't eat, that they look 'better' and might even get compliments, and this then distracts them from what really bothers them and gives them a new focus." Dahabra has helped several women who have developed dysfunctional eating behaviours after their husbands left them. "In one case the husband's parting words to her were a derogatory comment about her weight. She associated the breakup with being overweight, began dieting. She ended up being found unconscious at home and hospitalized because her blood sugar level had fallen very dangerously low."

Starving for Perfection

Dr Adrienne Key, the lead clinician for eating disorders treatment at the Priory clinic in Roehampton, southwest London, said: "In the last 18 months I've seen 10 women in their mid-to late-30s, mainly with bulimia, who have had a baby in the previous few years and have had increased body dissatisfaction. They start dieting but then try more drastic measures such as skipping meals or going on these strange protein, no-carbs diets, and then their starvation triggers the biology of an eating disorder."

Why only some women who do that then develop anorexia or bulimia is not fully understood, but it may be because their brains function slightly differently under the pressure of food deprivation, said Key. "Growing numbers of women in their 30s and 40s are dissatisfied with their bodies because they are presented with visual imagery of perfect bodies and unobtainable body ideals, especially in magazines, due to airbrushing, and they feel pressured to try to achieve that."

Mental health experts at the British Dietetic Association, which represents dieticians, have also noticed the same trend. Beat, the UK's [United Kingdom's] main eating disorders charity, is getting more calls from adults, mainly women.

Experts are unsure whether the growing number of older onset cases they are treating indicates a real change in people's behaviour or simply [general practitioners] becoming better at identifying eating disorders.

Men and Late-Onset Eating Disorders

Men can succumb too. Dahabra has treated one man who developed depression and then anorexia in his 40s amid grief at losing his mother. Another patient who was the same age was under severe stress, first at work, and then after losing his job and supporting his partner through a serious illness.

Lee Powell, a 37-year-old civil servant in Gloucester, saw his weight drop from over 10st [stone] to just over seven when obsessive exercise led him to start trying even harder to lose weight. "I used to have a cereal bar for breakfast and another for lunch, and then some proper food for my tea, but that quickly became just a salad. My wife, Annette, once said I looked like something out of a prisoner of war camp and broke down crying."

Experts are unsure whether the growing number of older onset cases they are treating indicates a real change in people's behaviour or simply GPs [general practitioners] becoming better at identifying eating disorders.

Struggle to Survive

By the time Natasha Craig died of anorexia in July 2007 at the age of 35, she weighed barely four stone. Years of starving herself had taken their toll. She fell over while playing with children at the primary school where she was a volunteer classroom assistant, broke two ribs and never recovered.

"She loved working at the school because the children didn't notice her thinness or comment on it," recalls her father Stuart. "After breaking the ribs her breathing got bad, she developed pneumonia and died soon." Anorexia, he points out, has the highest mortality rate of any mental illness, including depression, schizophrenia and bipolar disorder.

Natasha's struggle with anorexia since childhood proved so disabling that she grew to only five foot one; doctors said it should have been four inches more. It also led to her becoming stooped and developing severe osteoporosis, which seriously restricted the quality of her life. "Her legs were frail and she didn't have the stamina to walk very far; it became too painful for her," said Stuart.

"I think that anorexia is a bit like being an alcoholic, except that with alcohol it's much easier because you can give up drinking; but you can't give up eating."

While treatment exists for eating disorders, not all patients respond. That, says Stuart, helps explain why a third of anorexics are estimated to lead fairly normal lives, another third become seriously emaciated and the other third die.

VIEWPOINT 5

Misunderstanding Surrounds Late-Onset Eating Disorders in Canada

Sandy Naiman

Sandy Naiman is a journalist and blogger. In the following viewpoint, she describes her own experience with being diagnosed with an eating disorder at the age of sixty-two. Naiman contends that late-onset eating disorders may not be a new trend, but we are just more aware of the problem now. She attributes eating disorders to a combination of genetic and environmental factors and argues that they can be triggered by major life transitions and events. Naiman maintains that Canada needs to do a better job of providing treatment for older men and women affected by eating disorders.

As you read, consider the following questions:

1. According to the author, how far does the history of eating disorders go back?
2. How much does genetics account for developing anorexia or bulimia, according to Dr. Cynthia M. Bulik?
3. What does the author say is the average waiting time for an eating disorder assessment at Toronto General Hospital?

Sandy Naiman, "How I Got an Eating Disorder at 62," *Toronto Star*, August 4, 2011. www.thestar.com.

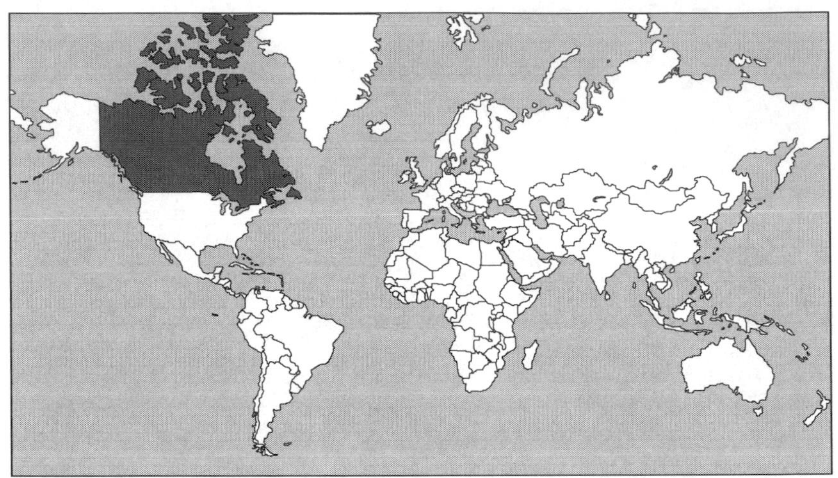

My morning ritual begins with a trip to the bathroom scale.

I strip off everything except my Medic Alert bracelet and step gingerly onto the glass and metal slab awaiting me.

Holding my breath, I glance down as my number comes up.

Phew. It's down from yesterday but up from last week when it dropped to my all-time low as an adult. Not good enough.

That number is my barometer, my forecast for the day. It dictates how I'll feel, but somehow, it's never quite good enough. I feel fat. I can't lose that feeling, even though I'm now wearing my 85 lb. kid sister's clothes.

I'm 62 and 5-ft. even. I've been an extreme yo-yo dieter my whole life, but it's growing harder and more oppressive every day.

"Stop dieting," people keep saying. "Stop losing." But I can't help it. I can't stop.

A New Trend?

Am I part of a so-called "new" phenomenon of middle-aged women with eating disorders that's increasingly reported in the media?

Actually, there is no new epidemic of eating disorders among people my age. But the public is only just beginning to comprehend that these illnesses—like all mental illnesses—don't discriminate. They're found in both sexes, all age groups, across diverse races and ethnic backgrounds and in countries all over the world.

"There is a huge amount of mythology about what eating disorders look like today," says Psych Central's associate editor Margarita Tartakovsky, a writer and blogger specializing in mental health, eating disorders and body image.

It's easy to blame the media, but that would be wrong, says Tartakovsky. The media and advertising undoubtedly perpetuate a culture of thinness that contributes to poor body image and body dissatisfaction, she says. But we can't really pin the blame for full-blown eating disorders on those glossy magazines and television commercials.

Disordered Eating vs. Eating Disorders

We can, however, hold them to account for what's known as disordered eating. The two are often confused. Disordered eating is defined as any sort of irregular eating behaviour that, while not exactly healthy, doesn't fit the characteristics required for an eating disorder diagnosis. Chances are good that you've observed disordered eating at some point while listening to a group of women agonize over restaurant menus.

If difficulties with eating start to interfere with a person's daily life, that's what makes it an actual eating disorder, says Blake Woodside, a psychiatrist specializing in adult eating disorders and medical director of the program for eating disorders at the Toronto General Hospital.

Some have referred to eating disorders in middle-aged women as "Desperate Housewives Syndrome," but experts say the term is not only insensitive but inaccurate.

Eating Disorders Have a Long History

Girls and women suffered from eating disorders long before the media existed. Their history dates back to ancient Greece with roots in religious fasting—women starving themselves as a form of self-flagellation, which still exists today.

That said, in the 1950s, sex icon Marilyn Monroe was 5-ft, 6-in. and weighed 135 lbs. By the 1970s, Jane Fonda—famous for popularizing aerobics—was 5-ft, 7-in. and 117 lbs. Obviously there's been a change in societal expectations, says Woodside.

Anorexia, bulimia and what are known as "eating disorders not otherwise specified (EDNOS)"—including binge eating disorder—are serious, potentially fatal mental illnesses, according to a 2011 report by the Academy for Eating Disorders (AED).

"Anorexia Nervosa (AN), in particular, has the highest mortality rate of any psychiatric disorder. Risk of premature death is 6–12 times higher in women with AN as compared to the general population," the AED report states.

Genes vs. Environment

Cynthia [M.] Bulik, PhD, director of the University of North Carolina eating disorders program, says, "Genetics account for over 50 per cent of liability to anorexia nervosa and the genetic contribution is similarly high for bulimia nervosa. Genetic factors also play a role in binge eating disorder. But, for all three, that means that it's not just genes—environment matters too."

"It's well accepted by leading researchers that eating disorders are genetically predisposed, tend to run in families and have nothing to do with metabolism," Tartakovsky says. "Anorexia nervosa and bulimia nervosa are psychiatric conditions, mental illnesses that need treatment."

But genetics are not black and white, and neuroscientists are learning more about how genetics work all the time, says Woodside.

While you have no control over your genetic risk, the latest research stresses that triggers are just as important.

"Furthermore, genes turn on and off all the time," Woodside explains. "Some genetic loading may be activated by dieting—this may be the most common environmental trigger—and other loading may be activated by other factors, such as the biological changes that occur in puberty."

Eating disorders at any age and in either gender develop because of the complex interplay of genetics and environment, experience or trauma.

Who's at Risk?

Girls and women, boys and men are at risk in countries where food is abundant, but the ratio is 10 women to every man.

Bulik says this unbalanced ratio might be due in part to the way we diagnose the disorders. In men, eating disorders may look different, "more of a drive toward muscularity. If we change the criteria a little, the ratio is not so discrepant. Binge eating disorder is not that different across the sexes."

Eating disorders at any age and in either gender develop because of the complex interplay of genetics and environment, experience or trauma.

"Let's say 10 girls go on a diet in the sixth grade. Nine of them will hate it and go out for ice cream on Saturday," Bulik explained. "For one it will be a calming, exhilarating experience that gives her a sense of control. Even though all these girls are exposed to the same environmental trigger, like a magazine that tells them to go on a diet, only for the one most genetically predisposed will it be a trigger for an eating disorder."

In her clinical practice, Bulik has seen adults with three manifestations of eating disorders. The illnesses can:

- Start in adolescence and persist through midlife
- Start in midlife
- Occur in adolescence, with a recovery period, then recur in midlife.

For science journalist and single mother Trisha Gura, PhD, 46, anorexia "gripped" her in her teens and she was unable, until recently, to let go and heal.

Though she had periods of recovery from the disease, the transitions of marriage, childbirth, divorce and even the completion of her 2007 groundbreaking annotated autobiography *Lying in Weight* sparked relapses. The following list is from her website.

15 Major Transitions That Can Trigger a Latent or First-Time Eating Disorder

- Becoming a grandparent
- Becoming a mother-in-law
- Experiencing an empty nest
- Having an empty nest filled by an adult child who's come home
- Returning to work
- Returning to school
- Caring for children and/or parents
- Suffering the death of a spouse
- Suffering the loss of or permanent separation from a child
- Divorce

- Remarriage
- Housing changes
- Retirement
- Chronic illness and disability
- Growing old and facing mortality

The watershed event that helped Gura get better was having a young daughter who was chubby when she hit puberty. "I didn't want to preach against obesity," Gura said. "I wanted to move to a better place in my life, to stop struggling, to accept myself."

Recovery

Gura went into treatment, a form of cognitive behaviour therapy. It took so much emotional strength, she says, to "give up the behaviours I'd relied on all my life and find new ones to take their place. For me, it was yoga, self-talk, and meditation."

Her French boyfriend is helping her develop a healthier relationship with food.

"He's shown me an entirely different culture around food. The way he relates to food is more normal than mine. You don't eat in your car. You don't feel guilty if you have a brownie. I find I'm eating without worrying about it. Food is not the centre of my life."

Still, old behaviours around food can remain an Achilles' heel [prominent weakness] for patients in recovery from eating disorders, Bulik says.

Like a recovered smoker who might crave a cigarette in times of stress, patients must be vigilant for the warning signs and enlist help from family or loved ones when thinking starts to get fuzzy as they approach a relapse. People with eating disorders can't always control stressors in their environments, but they can control their responses to them.

Addressing the Needs of Older Patients

Battling an eating disorder in midlife can pose significant challenges, the least of which may be attending group therapy with kids worried about going out for cheerleading. Fortunately, to address the increase in the numbers of older women seeking treatment, eating disorder facilities are beginning to develop counseling and treatment specifically geared toward this population's needs.

"Even though we do combine older and younger patients in group therapy, treatment needs to be developmentally appropriate, so we've created a separate track which focuses on issues unique to our older patients," says Adrienne Ressler, national training director for the Renfrew Center Foundation and board president of the International Association of Eating Disorders Professionals.

Cathy Leman,
"Binge Eating, Purging—and Aging,"
Miller-McCune, *November 5, 2009.*

There Is Hope

Eating disorders are among the most fatal of all mental illnesses, though anorexia is highly treatable, especially with early intervention, Woodside says.

These disorders are obsessions. They are not choices. They're an irresistible urge to behave in a certain way, against your conscious wishes.

The addiction is to the behaviour of dieting, not the food, explains Woodside.

"It's a cruel deception to expect people just to live with these eating disorders when they are so treatable without drug intervention," he says. "But it takes time."

"Eating disorders are complex mental illnesses, but there's hope for middle-aged women," he said.

"We get excellent results in older women—not every time, but we do get good results, often enough to keep on trying."

These disorders are obsessions. They are not choices. They're an irresistible urge to behave in a certain way, against your conscious wishes.

Access to Treatment

Both Bulik and Woodside say they are upset by the shortage of clinics and psychiatrists and psychologists treating eating disorders because they are misperceived as illnesses only affecting adolescent girls and young women.

"I see Canada is no better than we are in getting people in when they need help. It is a sad, sad situation—and the worst part of my job!" Bulik says.

Woodside went into a rant. "If more people knew that eating disorders affect men and women, there would be eating disorder clinics in every hospital."

The average waiting time for an assessment is now four months at Toronto General Hospital.

As for my personal situation, three months after being referred by my psychiatrist, I've just been assessed by the eating disorders clinic at Toronto General Hospital. I've been given a workbook to start helping myself at home, but I don't yet know when my treatment will start.

American Researchers Are Investigating Picky Eating Syndrome

Julia Belluz

Julia Belluz is a journalist. In the following viewpoint, she looks at recent attempts of researchers exploring the eating disorder of picky eating, which is widespread with children but can also be found in adults. For people with this disorder, food may actually taste differently than it does for other people and can lead to severe food restrictions. This phenomenon can result in profound social, professional, and health problems, Belluz explains. Researchers have launched an American registry for picky eaters, the Finicky Eating in Adults study, which aims to gather information on the disorder.

As you read, consider the following questions:

1. What food does the author say that most picky eating adults have in their limited food repertoire?
2. What do many picky eaters in America call Thanksgiving, according to the author?
3. What does Marsha D. Marcus say is the difference between picky eaters and people with food quirks?

Julia Belluz, "The Plight of Picky Eating Adults," *Maclean's*, July 20, 2010. www2.macleans.ca.

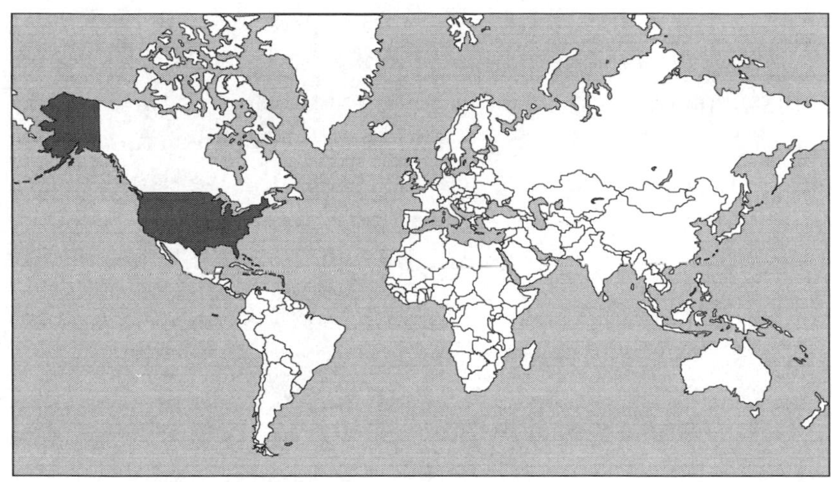

Rhonda West's picky eating began during breastfeeding. "I couldn't have my mother's milk, so they put me on cow's milk, but I was allergic, so then they put me on soy," she says. "When it came time for solid foods, I didn't want any part of that." In fact, most foods made her want to gag.

Now, 41 years later, West is a picky eating adult. She survives on toast, waffles, pancakes, simply cooked meats, and French fries. (Oddly, almost all adult "selective eaters" include French fries in their limited food repertoire.) "I don't like foods that are mixed-up together," says West, who lives in the Washington, DC, area and is currently looking for work. No vegetables, few fruits, and absolutely nothing that's too soft or squishy. "I equate eating pasta with eating a plate of worms."

For picky eaters, most meals are unbearable, and nearly all foods make them nauseous; failed relationships, lost work opportunities, and anxiety caused by the very thing others derive great pleasure from.

Acknowledging the Problem

While childhood picky eating is commonly recognized, little has been done to understand people like West—until now. In July [2010], Duke University and the University of Pittsburgh launched the first national public registry of picky eaters, known as the Finicky Eating in Adults study. People can log in and complete a survey about their relationship with food and eating habits. It's still [in its] early stages, but this study is designed to help researchers better understand "avoidant, restrictive food intake disorder"—which is currently under consideration as an officially recognized eating disorder, like bulimia or anorexia.

For picky eaters, most meals are unbearable, and nearly all foods make them nauseous.

Marsha D. Marcus, chief of the behavioral medicine program at the University of Pittsburgh Medical Center and one of the lead investigators on the study, says picky eaters tend to fall into one of three groups: those with taste issues, those who have never had a real interest in food, and a third group who have had traumatic or aversive experiences with food.

Marcus says it's too early to tell how many suffer from this disorder, but she's heard of cases where one's eating restrictions are so acute they survive by a feeding tube. Others avoid vacations, business meetings, dinner parties, and weddings—any event that brings them into contact with unknown food. Indeed, one American sufferer said that Thanksgiving is known among picky eaters as "Black Thursday."

However, Marcus is careful to distinguish adult picky eaters from people with the food quirks most everybody lives with. "We're not trying to pathologize people's preferences," she says. "We're looking for people whose food restrictions are a source of impairment or distress or have led to a health problem."

A Genetic Link?

One interesting theory the researchers will explore is whether picky eating is genetic. "There might be a group of people

> **What Drives Picky Eating?**
>
> Researchers don't know yet what drives the behavior [of picky eating], but they say textures and smell can account for a picky eater's limited diet. Some will only eat foods with one consistent texture or one taste, leading some medical experts to speculate that picky eaters have some obsessive-compulsive tendencies.
>
> *Shirley S. Wang,*
> *"No Age Limit on Picky Eating,"*
> Wall Street Journal, *July 5, 2010.*

who have different ways of tasting, so the food that tastes good to you or me tastes awful to them," says Marcus.

According to picky eater West, this is a distinct possibility. "Picky eating is nature not nurture," West says. "People are light, sound, smell, touch, skin sensitive—why not taste?" In fact, West insists that if she could change her palate, she would. "It's high anxiety when you're going to meet new people, especially for a job, and you have to explain why you're not eating anything on the menu," she says. When she summons the courage to go to a restaurant, she usually requests plain grilled chicken.

Canada's Pickiest Eater

T.J. Haselden, a computer salesman living in Montreal, refers to himself as "the pickiest eater in Canada." Of the disorder, the part-time comedian says, "I have learned to laugh about it, but the truth is that I'm really getting fed up."

Haselden eats only six foods: hot dogs, hamburgers, chicken, turkey, bacon, and French fries. He gags at the thought of tasting anything new, and also claims that this disorder began in childhood. "Everybody tries to say it's my mom's fault for not treating it the right way. I always say the only thing I can blame my mom for is that she was too accommodating."

When he was a teenager living with roommates, Haselden would stay away from the kitchen. When friends ordered pizza, he'd tell them he was allergic to tomatoes to avoid confrontation. Now 30, he lives with his wife, Chantal, and has realized that his picky eating infringes on her life, too. "She can't explore her taste buds the way she would want to." For example, when she eats something as simple as pasta—a dish he abhors—the two have to sit at opposite ends of the dinner table. "I can smell the pasta so much I feel like I could taste it and it makes me want to gag."

Haselden is undertaking a film project in the hopes that he can broaden his palate. He'll document a 30-day journey of new tastes, attempting to try every food he's been afraid of. "I want to use the power of the camera to overcome my fear and make people laugh."

Developing a Treatment Program for Picky Eaters

But can he and other picky eaters change their ways? Nancy Zucker, the director of the Duke Center for Eating Disorders who is leading the study with Marcus, says she hopes so. Her goal is to come up with effective coping strategies and treatment, and to distinguish selective eating from other eating disorders.

"People have a tough time having empathy for those who taste things differently," she observes. "Even more profoundly, imagine you had an experience and you tasted something and thought, 'this tastes like cardboard' and people were mad at you for that, saying that you're not experiencing what you're experiencing. That's what these people go through every day. It's time we explore and recognize what's going on here."

Periodical and Internet Sources Bibliography

The following articles have been selected to supplement the diverse views presented in this chapter.

Daniel Bates	"Fussy Eaters Could Be Classed as Having an Eating Disorder," *Daily Mail* (UK), July 9, 2010.
Anita Chaudhuri	"The New Eating Disorders," *Sunday Times* (London), June 27, 2010.
Dan Even	"Can Too Much Healthy Food Hurt You?," *Haaretz* (Israel), January 1, 2009.
Emma Gray	"Orthorexia: Too Much of a Healthy Thing?," *Huffington Post*, August 26, 2011. www.huffingtonpost.com.
Amelia Hill	"Healthy Food Obsession Sparks Rise in New Eating Disorder," *Observer* (UK), August 15, 2009.
Bonnie Rochman	"Orthorexia: Can Healthy Eating Be a Disorder?," *Time*, February 12, 2010.
Sara Shea	"Nature vs. Nurture: The Media's Effect on Body Image," *The River Reporter* (blog), May 8, 2009. http://theriverreporter.wordpress.com.
Erin Skarda	"Does Extremely Picky Eating in Adulthood Signal a Mental Disorder?," *Healthland* (blog), December 3, 2010. http://healthland.time.com.
Amanda Ursell	"My Son Has a Diet Fetish," *Times* (London), March 29, 2011.
Shirley S. Wang	"No Age Limit on Picky Eating," *Wall Street Journal*, July 5, 2010.

Chapter 2

Body Image and Eating Disorders

Viewpoint 1

Argentina Has the Second Highest Rate of Eating Disorders in the World

Lindsey Hoshaw

Lindsey Hoshaw is a reporter for the Argentina Independent. *In the following viewpoint, she underscores Argentina's problem with eating disorders, reporting that next to Japan, it has more citizens with these disorders than any other country. Hoshaw contends that although an obsession with beauty and being thin exists in a number of South American countries, Argentina researches and reports on the problem, making it more transparent. The Argentine government has taken steps to address the high rate of eating disorders, including laws to carry larger sizes in stores, Hoshaw maintains. There are also organizations such as the Association Against Bulimia and Anorexia (ALUBA) that are determined to help as many men and women as possible.*

As you read, consider the following questions:

1. According to ALUBA, how many Argentines have eating disorders?
2. How many Argentines out of ten have undergone plastic surgery, according to the *Guardian*?

Lindsey Hoshaw, "Starving for Perfection," *Argentina Independent*, June 27, 2008. www.argentinaindependent.com.

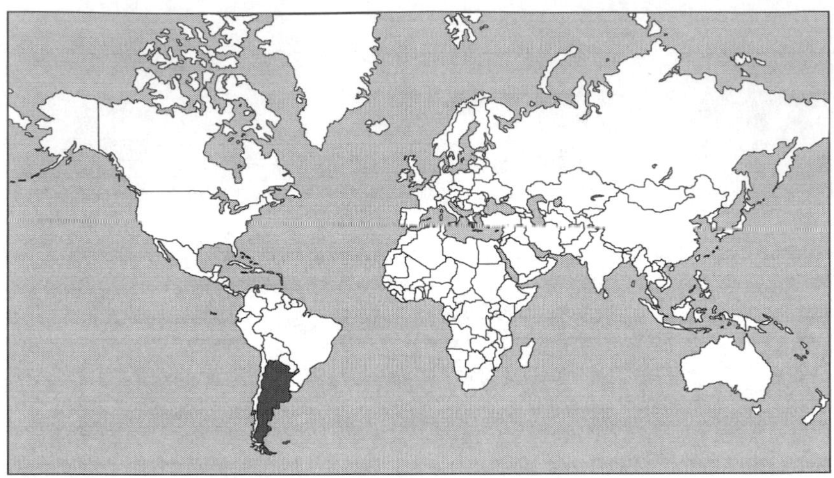

3. What does the law of sizes require, according to the author?

Two years ago, Julieta Paus couldn't consume anything without counting the calories. "For lunch I chewed gum and drank *mate* [a beverage made by steeping dried leaves in hot water], but nothing else," the 18-year-old said. "I felt bad even after drinking *mate*, so I'd run to the bathroom to get rid of it."

Paus is one of millions of Argentines who struggle with an eating disorder. According to the Association Against Bulimia and Anorexia (ALUBA), one in ten Argentines has the illness, which translates to four million people nationwide. After Japan, Argentina has more citizens with the disorder than any other country.

Anorexia nervosa and bulimia are the two most common types of eating disorders. Symptoms of anorexia nervosa include a relentless pursuit to be thin and unnatural eating behaviours such as deliberate self-starvation, according to the National Institute of Mental Health. Bulimia nervosa is characterised by binging followed by purging—usually vomiting, fasting, excessive exercise or intake of diuretics.

What Factors Drive Eating Disorders?

Cultural factors like eating and smoking habits may also be contributing to the incidence of eating disorders. At any given time 30% of *porteñas* [natives of Buenos Aires] are dieting and 33.5% of adults smoke, according to the *Albion Monitor* and the Ministry of Health. Women with the disorder often use smoking to suppress their appetite and increase their metabolism. Smoking burns up to 200 calories a day and slightly increases a person's metabolism. Nicotine also acts as an appetite suppressant, so many women fear gaining weight if they quit.

Paus' binge anorexia, which is characterised by restrictive eating followed by vomiting, started in 2002 after her mother passed away from a malignant brain tumour. Paus soon experienced depression and panic attacks. She said during the past two years her illness intensified and she wasn't able to finish school.

"When I went out in public I felt fine," the high school student said. "But I wasn't. I was sick and it took five people, from doctors to my friends to my dad, to make me realise I had a problem."

Paus who has now been at the ALUBA, the largest anorexia and bulimia clinic in Buenos Aires, for nine months, looks healthy and said she is in [transition]. "I am learning to have meals in public," Paus said. "I used to eat alone, but I'm learning how to share, to chat."

Argentina's Beauty Obsession

Dr Mabel Bello, founder of the clinic, said Argentina has an aesthetic obsession. "The women here don't want to look old and plastic surgery is very common," Bello said.

One in 30 Argentines is estimated to have gone under the knife, according to the *Guardian*. This makes the country the most operated on in the world after the US and México.

Bello, who opened the centre in 1986 hoping to give women hope for the future, said society is largely influential. "The culture is sick," the psychologist said. "Globally everyone wants to look the same, to be thin, to be attractive. Family values disappear and girls grow up without a sense of security."

Bello pointed out that other countries in South America had just as many unrealistic expectations about their body image. "I've worked in Peru and Uruguay and the problem is just as serious," Bello said. "But the women don't want to be included in research studies. There are more statistics about Argentina so it seems like it's a bigger problem than in other countries."

The principal causes of anorexia and bulimia are low self-esteem combined with a poor body image, a genetic predisposition, influences from the media and behaviours learned from family members.

Warning Signs

The principal causes of anorexia and bulimia are low self-esteem combined with a poor body image, a genetic predisposition, influences from the media and behaviours learned from family members.

According to the [American Psychiatric Association], people with anorexia nervosa and bulimia tend to be perfectionists who suffer from low self-esteem and are extremely critical of themselves and their bodies. "Some people are weaker and some are stronger than others," said ALUBA psychologist Ricardo de Leon. "Usually people [with an eating disorder] think life is too difficult so this is a coping mechanism."

The [American Psychiatric Association] also points out that anorexic women usually 'feel fat' and see themselves as overweight, sometimes despite life-threatening malnutrition.

De Leon added that there is often a genetic predisposition. "It's a pathological illness like depression, addiction or a phobia."

Family dynamics play a pivotal role, Bello added. "Today there isn't good communication between parents and their kids. They are more influenced by TV and all of a sudden the body becomes very important."

The Internet has also played a large role with pro-anorexia websites popping up to encourage self-deprivation. One blog called *Light as a Feather Thin as a Rail* offers tips on how to lose weight instantly.

The tagline reads like an infomercial: 'Preoccupied with getting and staying thin? Interested in pro-ana tips, thinspiration, fasting, celebrity weight loss secrets, effective diet pills, effective diets, exercise equipment and exercise DVDs? If you Like What You Read, Buy Me A Fat Free Café Latte! Hugs & Kisses!!!'

The Internet has also played a large role with pro-anorexia websites popping up to encourage self-deprivation.

The Law Intervenes

Three years ago Argentina passed the law of sizes (ley de talles) requiring stores to stock larger sizes. The law, which was put into effect in December 2005, mandates that all stores in the Buenos Aires province carry sizes equivalent to UK [United Kingdom] 10–20. Clothing manufacturers, importers and distributors had half a year's notice, and businesses that don't comply could face a $450,000 fine or even closure.

But Argentines are sceptical about the actual enforcement of the law. Lawyer Maria Eugenia Urbani, 25, said it is still difficult to find clothes that fit.

"Being 1.73m [metres] and weighing 69kg [kilograms] makes it impossible to buy a pair of jeans in Buenos Aires.

Size Discrimination in Argentina

According to Monique Altschul, the executive director of the feminist organisation Fundación Mujeres en Igualdad (Women in Equality Foundation), approximately 70% [of] Argentine women have difficulty finding clothes that fit. As a result, women have no choice but to shop at specialty stores that carry larger sizes, but in Argentina, fashion and larger sizes are not congruous.

Sharon Haywood,
"Battling the Beauty Myth in Argentina,"
AnyBody, July 6, 2010. http://anybody.squarespace.com.

The remedy? Either buying tight pants and stretching them for two weeks until you show yourself out in the real world, or buy in less trendy brands that usually have larger sizes."

De Leon agreed that the laws may not be fully enforced. "A lot of stores don't comply but of course it's a good idea. Everyone should have the right to buy clothes that fit their bodies."

"It's very arbitrary how they do the sizes," Bello added. "It doesn't correspond to real people so they change their bodies to fit the clothes." The ALUBA founder said the benefit of the law is the consciousness it raises about Argentina's obsession with thinness.

"The fact that we need laws to tell fashion designers and shops that they have to design 'larger' sizes shows just how pathetic and aesthetically oriented our society is," Urbani said.

Reclaiming a Balance

In addition to the law of sizes, some international companies like Dove have taken it upon themselves to change the way we think. Their 'Campaign for Real Beauty' has created a series of advertisements promoting attractive non-models and debunking beauty myths. On their 60-second 'The Evolution of Beauty' commercial, they show how a model is transformed through Photoshop.

The commercial shows the woman having her hair and makeup done over several hours. Her image is later changed through a computer programme—her neck is elongated, her jawline is slimmed down and her eyes are enlarged. The final image ends up on a billboard near a car park. The message that appears on the screen before the end of the commercial reads: 'No wonder our perception of beauty is so distorted'.

Clinics like ALUBA are also working to instill healthy expectations about weight and beauty. Over the past 22 years the centre has helped over 20,000 patients. They offer free counselling sessions and group meetings for parents. The centre focuses on teaching patients the causes and signs of their illness and the genetic link. Through group sessions, patients are surrounded by their peers and learn to talk openly about their struggles.

Though the majority of patients are between the ages of 15 and 25, ALUBA's youngest patients are four years old. At this age most of the influence comes from the parents. "Often mothers say they want to be skinny and their children internalise it." Bello said. She asserted that every person has a right to feel comfortable in their own body. "Eating disorders rob a person of their dreams for the future. Women aren't allowed to feel life, to love, to feel healthy. It's one of the biggest problems of the century."

Viewpoint 2

The Incredible Shrinking Model

Emily Nussbaum

Emily Nussbaum is a contributing editor to New York *magazine. In the following viewpoint, she contends that fashion models are susceptible to developing eating disorders because of the immense pressure placed on them to stay thin by a demanding, competitive industry. Nussbaum notes that things in the fashion world have changed since the 1980s and 1990s, when supermodels were stars and had more realistic body images. Today, models have less power, are replaceable and disposable, and feel more pressure to conform to unrealistic body weight, in Nussbaum's view.*

As you read, consider the following questions:

1. According to Nussbaum, what are the regular sample sizes from designers today?
2. How much does the author say a top model can make during New York Fashion Week?
3. What designer called fashion industry guidelines to prevent eating disorders "politically correct Fascism," according to the author?

To view this article in its entirety, please visit http://nymag.com/fashion/07/spring/28149/.

Backstage at the Carlos Miele show, all the accents are Russian. The models are rubbing off makeup, having transformed from Miele's glamorous jet-setters back into harried teenagers. They look skinny but not cadaverous. Yet after a week in the Bryant Park tents, I realize I can't trust my own judgment: It's already become impossible to see the difference between thin and *thin*.

I walk up to Nataliya Gotsii, who grimaces when I ask her about new industry guidelines on eating disorders. Everyone at Fashion Week makes this face when I raise the subject: After a year of media coverage criticizing the size-zero model, fashion has gotten tired of explaining itself. But Gotsii has particular reason to worry. She was one of the models whose photos have been used to illustrate the controversy—a shot of her ribs was flashed on CNN in order to elicit shocked reactions from celebrities.

"It's all about the Ukrainian models," she tells me with frustration. "After last Fashion Week, I hear a lot about myself, in the news! I didn't come back here for two months because clients refused to work with me. Me and Snejana and the other Ukrainian models." All of the runway models are thin, she points out, and she wonders why she was singled out. "Maybe, some of the girls, they skinny, but they look natural? Some of the girls, they don't look healthy?"

Her mother cried when she saw those pictures, says Gotsii. But her body was Photoshopped, she claims. Those circles under her eyes (and I can see them: pale-brown half-moons) are genetic—her brother has them, too. "Nobody cares, they just take a name and put a lot of shit. We're going out, we're having dinners, everybody's eating, there's no anorexia in this business!"

It's not true, of course. A week after our conversation, a perilously thin teenage model, Eliana Ramos, would die in Uruguay, apparently of a heart attack, making it three model deaths in the past seven months. In August, Ramos's older sister Luisel died after restricting herself to a diet of lettuce leaves and Diet Coke. In November, Brazilian model Ana Carolina Reston died weighing just 88 pounds.

But Gotsii resents being dragged into the debate. In those notorious pictures from last season, she had worn a white halter top dangling from chains; you could count her vertebrae. In a taupe bikini she stood, hands on hips, staring into the camera, a tanned skeleton.

If she looked so terrible, if she looked run-down, it had nothing to do with food, she argues. Already today Gotsii has walked in two shows, and she has another one scheduled for tonight. Her first fitting had begun at 6:30 a.m. Next week, she's off to Paris, then Milan. "You live for almost one month just about fashion. Fashion, fashion, fashion—it makes you tired in the head. In two weeks, maybe I will look tired again."

I look at her and try to remember the pictures I've seen. Does she look too thin? She's not wearing a bikini right now, so I can't tell. She looks fine, if a little tired.

And then she looks me in the eye and asks, "I'm not so scary, am I?"

Raise the issue of eating disorders during Fashion Week, and someone will inevitably bring up that lost, glorious era of the supermodel: Christy, Naomi, Cindy, Linda, the four-headed stompy-legged beast with big shiny hair, the one that wouldn't get up for less than $10,000. Those were the days when models took up space. They were stars. They made demands. And their faces were everywhere. To paraphrase from *Sunset Boulevard*, sometimes it feels like it's not the clothes that have gotten small, it's the models. (Although, of course, the clothes have shrunk, too, sample sizes dwindling from a 6 to a 4 to a 2 and below.)

These days, fashion people do not talk about models with awe. Instead, they speak of them with condescending affection, as if they were lovable circus folk. Again and again, I hear that they are "beautiful freaks," "genetic anomalies"—girls born to be bone-thin, with giraffe-like necks and the wide, pretty doll faces that are the latest visual sensation. But there is also pity for the models, who are, many peoplc pointed out to me, basically high school dropouts, teenagers from poor countries, whose careers last a very short time. They are infinitely replaceable. Although top girls can make up to $100,000 in a week of shows, the vast majority get nowhere near that; some of the more prominent designers pay the girls only in clothes.

These days, fashion people do not talk about models with awe. Instead, they speak of them with condescending affection, as if they were lovable circus folk.

In the great anorexia debate, models are talked about but rarely heard. Which is why it was so startling when Natalia Vodianova, one of those great and silent beautiful ones, the Cinderella from Russia, rose to speak at the Council of Fashion Designers of America panel on eating disorders. It was Monday, the first day of Fashion Week, at 8 a.m. There was an air of anticlimax in the room, since the group's guidelines—released to the media weeks before—had already been picked apart like a chicken sandwich. Whereas Madrid and Milan had passed rules barring models whose body mass index fell below 18 and 18.5, respectively, the U.S. organization presented nonbinding suggestions. Designers should offer healthy food backstage, eliminate drinking, and ban smoking. They should stop using models under 16 and should not keep them up past midnight (a suggestion that made the girls sound a bit like gremlins). The guidelines seemed at once a good first step and a bit of preemptive ass-covering, but even these mild suggestions were unlikely to stick: Could an industry devoted to unrealistic standards of beauty really recognize an eating disorder, let alone prevent one? Already, designers like Karl Lagerfeld were grumbling about "politically correct Fascism."

Things proceeded with muted goodwill for half an hour. There was Dr. Susan Ice, the medical director of the Renfrew Center, an eating-disorder-treatment organization, who emphasized that these were "biopsychosocial illnesses" rooted in childhood and genetics. Fitness guru David Kirsch pledged to "educate, enlighten, and empower all." Joy Bauer, the nutritionist for the New York City Ballet, offered workshops to debunk weight-loss myths and teach models "to eat for increased energy levels, for optimal beauty, for better skin, hair, teeth, muscle tone, debloating—things that I know they're interested in."

Then Vodianova stood up, with her sad and enormous eyes, her beautiful wide face familiar from the cover of *Vogue* and ads for Calvin Klein. She began by quoting Oscar Wilde: "'To love oneself is the beginning of a lifelong romance'—a very wonderful and inspired saying. But I hope you will agree that no relationship comes that easy.

"I come from a poor background," Vodianova told the carefully vetted crowd of fashionistas and their critics. Anna Wintour sat to her right, face concealed by the familiar bob. "I ate because I wanted to stay alive, and it never occurred to me to think of food in any other way." In 2000, when she arrived in Paris at the age of 17, she discovered that her fellow models were obsessed with weight. "At first I kind of sneered, thinking that this would never affect me. But as I began working, I began paying attention to my body shape for the first time. . . . Eating was secondary. But I found a lot of new friends who were living the same lifestyle, and things were far too exciting to worry about it."

At 19, Vodianova gave birth to a son and quickly became skinnier than ever, impressing the fashion world. At five-nine, she weighed only 106 pounds, her hair was thinning, she was anxious and depressed—and she was a runway star with her first major advertising contract. After a friend confronted her, she sought help and got healthier, adding on a few pounds. But when she got up to 112 pounds, her agent sat her down: Designers were complaining she wasn't as thin as she used to be. "I defended myself, saying it was crazy to consider measurements like 33-27-34 to be normal. I think because I was one of the girls most in demand it helped me to be able to forget the incident quickly. On the other hand, it makes me think that if I had been weak at the time, I can really imagine how it could have helped me endanger myself."

The models she had met on her way to the top, she told the audience, were more malleable. "They were very young, a lot of them were very lonely, far from home and their loved ones. Most came from poor backgrounds and were helping their families. They left their childhood behind with dreams of a better life, and for most of them, there was nothing they wouldn't do to live those dreams."

All through Fashion Week, the models told me they felt persecuted by the media conversation, as if they were being blamed for their bodies.

"You know, I don't sing because I don't have the voice," said Flavia, 22, with a sigh. "If I don't have this body, I could not be a model. I eat like a pig!"

"I'm this kind of person who can eat whatever I want," echoed Eva. "I'm so happy that I still can eat ice cream and everything."

"There's always going to be that one somebody who has taken it too far," Sophie told me. I asked her if she knew of anybody who had. No, she said. "All the girls in my model apartment eat everything. We stuff our faces."

But another model, Marvy Rieder, told me she had no patience for that kind of talk. "It's b.s.," she said flatly on the phone from the Netherlands, where she was busily packing for

Modeling
Agency
"YOU HAVE POTENTIAL, BUT YOU
NEED TO LOSE SOME WEIGHT."

"You have potential, but you need to lose some weight," cartoon by Mike Artell, www.CartoonStock.com. Copyright © Mike Artell. Reproduction rights obtainable from www.CartoonStock.com.

a photo shoot in Zambia. A Dutch model who has worked to educate the public on the subject of eating disorders, Rieder beat out 20,000 girls to be the face of Guess watches. Then she came to New York, where she was told that if she wanted to do runway work, she needed to lose weight. She dieted and exercised, but that wasn't sufficient.

"I started skipping things. I was still eating, but not enough, *really* not enough, and going to the gym every day." Her roommates in the model apartment were eating a can of corn a day, Rieder said. "Or an apple. Or whatever. And that's just one of the things I've seen." I asked Rieder if models are open about restricting food. No, she told me. "They hide it. By saying, 'I just ate so much at home, I'm not hungry anymore.' I've heard it a million times."

Why do models not speak out about these issues? "In my opinion, I think it's because they're afraid of losing work," said Rieder.

Sabrina Hunter, 27, agrees. I found the gorgeous Afro-Caribbean woman not strutting the catwalk but working the Cingular booth in the pavilion outside. She'd left runway modeling, she told me, because the pressure was so intense that it required her to eat in a disordered way. At five-ten, Hunter was expected to be "115 or lower, preferably." After she signed with an American agency, she was given a choice: Lose weight or gain and be a plus-size model. After trying to gain unsuccessfully, she went the opposite direction, eating 600 calories and jogging five miles a day. "It made me extremely moody and depressed. And I looked it, in the face. But that's how all the models look," she says.

Both Rieder and Hunter have known models who are naturally skinny. But many of these girls are exceptionally young: A model who is effortlessly flat-chested and hipless at 14 will start to struggle as she hits her late teens. If she's already rising in the industry, she may find that she needs to take more extreme measures to continue to fit the bony aesthetic. And that goes double for the new breed of models, many of whom come, like Vodianova, from the poorest regions of Eastern Europe. For these girls, pressures to stay thin may be a small price to pay for escaping the small towns they came from.

"One of the interesting things about these models today is that they get used and spit out so quickly," says Magali Amadei, a model who has been open about her recovery from bulimia. "The era of the supermodel is over, so girls working today don't have the earning power. These girls come into the business young, and they are disposable. On top of that, people often talk about your appearance in front of you, as if you can't hear them."

Such pressures can be the most intense on girls who walk the runway, a job that possesses a strange, catch-22 quality. Models must not distract from the clothes, and yet their chance to succeed is to stand out. If she gets noticed, a model can grab the big prize—a major ad campaign. These contracts offer financial security and celebrity, which translates to a modicum of power, although nothing compared with the days when models rather than celebrities commanded the covers of fashion magazines.

"It's a far more complex issue than people realize," Suzy Menkes, the fashion writer for the *International Herald Tribune*, told me. "You know, many of these girls were brought up in the post-Communist years on an extremely bad diet. From childhood, they've not been properly nourished. That may make them very appealing to designers, but they don't start off with a healthy body. And nothing is simple. I think it must be incredibly difficult to come from a vegetable stall in the Ukraine and find yourself in Paris amongst Ladurée macaroons. People have to accept that it's a much bigger picture than terrible fashion folk starving to get into frocks."

Models must not distract from the clothes, and yet their chance to succeed is to stand out. If she gets noticed, a model can grab the big prize—a major ad campaign.

Backstage at Vera Wang, I run into Tanya Dziahileva, who might as well be the younger version of Natalia Vodianova. She's 15 years old and has been working since she was 14. She's from Belarus. Vodianova had described herself as wearing "some kind of pink glasses" when she began modeling, and I can see that Tanya is wearing them too. After days of watching metronomic struts and thousand-yard stares, I realize she's the first model I've really seen smile. It's not just a smile, either: She is beaming with excitement, her words pouring out of her like Champagne.

"The models is *models*, it's not like normal people, you know? They have to be beautiful, with good skin, and everything perfect." The girls who got sick, she thinks, "were just models who were so stupid, to don't eat food, you know? You have to eat good! I eat gorgeous food. I eat sushi, I eat meat, I eat steaks. I eat more than you, I'm sure.

"You know, it's actually really nice, that people take care about the models," she says softly, when I tell her about the CFDA guidelines, which would ban her from the catwalk. "But I'm 15 years old and I feel like I can do this. And I don't want to stop it! I don't want to stop it for one month, I don't want to stop it for one day. Some girls, you know, they look so young, and so, I don't know—I feel that I need to come to their home and help them go to sleep! But I can't say I feel like I'm 15. I feel like I'm 20. I feel like I'm 30! Because I feel great. My life is gorgeous! Who at 15 years old can see all the world, you know? It's just incredible, it's beautiful, it's amazing, it's—Fashion World!"

On Thursday of fashion week, I went to the far West Village to see Marchesa, the label designed by Harvey Weinstein's . . . girlfriend? (No one can finish the sentence for me.) There was no runway. Instead, the models were perched around the space in live tableaux: one of them balanced on a spiral staircase above a reflecting pool; others standing in pairs, gazing above the heads of the guests, like a glamorous variation on the Buckingham Palace guards.

It was awkward, and accidentally funny, to act as if the models standing three feet away from us were mannequins. André Leon Talley strode through, gesturing at the outfits, shouting "You must buy all of these!" at a pretty socialite he was steering by the elbow. A handsome young man walked straight up to a model and looked her up and down. The moment felt uncomfortably erotic—she couldn't move, he could—but then he seemed embarrassed and moved away, back to his girlfriend, and they laughed.

If Fashion Week is about reinforcing hierarchies, skinniness has always been a way to compete. Being thin means control and, symbolically, that you are rich, that you are young, that you are beautiful, that you are powerful. And yet the models themselves, who are skinnier and younger than anyone, seem like the weakest people here: manual laborers with short shelf lives. And whatever their eating habits, the girls in the gowns attract, like anorexics, an unstable mix of envy, anxiety, and scorn, a cultural response reserved for women reduced (or maybe elevated) to their bodies.

And for observers of the catwalk, there remains the nagging question: Why this skinny? Why now? Why are designers casting bodies that are, if not actively anorexic, practically indistinguishable from the girls at Renfrew?

I hear two dominant theories. The first is that fashion is aspirational. There's makeup; there's lighting; it is intended to be extreme, not realistic—to inspire envy, by providing a vision of an impossible life the audience member would love to live. One editor I spoke with wondered if the tiny socialites, the demographic that can afford these expensive garments, naturally prefer to see even tinier girls on the runway, so they could have something to aspire to. According to this theory, we would all love to be that thin.

The other theory is that the girls need to be skinny because they need to be invisible. Clothing stands out best when the body is a blank. And the better the clothes are, the more extreme the skinniness must be. Certainly, the glittering sacks that many designers are featuring these days flatter only a body that recedes inside them (like the Mary-Kate Olsen look, these puffy garments have an unnerving resemblance to the extra-large sweatshirts I remember anorexics wearing back in college).

"Models are quote-unquote hangers," points out Kate Armenta, the booker for *Vogue*—although she is also eager to detach her own publication from any responsibility for this issue. "Honestly, I have to give credit to Anna," she tells me. "She's always been very outspoken against thin models. *Vogue* has never tried to perpetuate that look." (A perusal of the magazine would seem to indicate otherwise.)

But, of course, these two explanations are diametrically opposed. In the first vision, the models must be thin so people look at them. In the second, they must be thin so that no one will notice them. And when I ask the buyers and the customers, they seem baffled about the reason for it all.

"Our clients aren't this thin!" says Lance Lawson, the owner and buyer for Jake, a high-end designer store in Chicago. When you see the actual runway samples, he adds, "it looks like children's clothing. We'll say, 'What size is this?' and even in the showroom they laugh: 'Oh, that's not a size.'"

The truth is, no one really has a good explanation for the change. The sophisticated fashion observer notes that this is just how fashion works: The Gibson girl gives way to the flapper, then to the big-shouldered forties girl and her busty fifties counterpart, and on to Twiggy, the eighties Amazons, Kate Moss, the waifs, and heroin chic—and for the past ten years, thinner and thinner, younger and younger, in what can feel like some sort of terrifying endgame. Celebrity culture has added its own catalyst, that parade of starlets dwindling competitively in *US Weekly*. Women's bodies have always been theater, and this is just another act.

Fashion historian Valerie Steele wonders if this isn't the flip side of the obesity crisis: "As everyone is blimping up, we're idealizing thinness. It can't be separated." But unlike many fashion observers, Steele isn't willing to acknowledge that models are especially thin at all—or, if they are, that it's the outside world's business. "When there's a thin actress or singer, no one says we have to fatten up actresses and singers!

No, it's fashion that's the whipping boy. You know: 'It's so criminal that fashion employs underage girls in the Third World!'" she argues. "Well, so does the electronics industry."

That's true, of course. It's all true: that gymnasts get eating disorders, too, that Hollywood is also a problem, and why aren't we talking about world hunger instead? But finally, the conversation shrinks to a tautology: The clothes are on very thin girls, so clothes must look best on very thin girls. And there are questions it is hard to ask in Fashion World, too bumptious and too basic: Aren't clothes intended to flatter those who purchase them? What kind of message does this send to young women? And, the electronics industry aside, isn't there something a little creepy about using teenage girls from poor countries to model gowns that get bought mainly by incredibly wealthy adult women? . . .

Viewpoint 3

Eating Disorders Rising Problem Among Orthodox Jews

Associated Press

The Associated Press is an American news organization. In the following viewpoint, the reporter maintains that eating disorders are a serious, underdiagnosed disease in the Orthodox Jewish community. A big part of the problem is that the community sends a mixed message: Young women are pressured to be thin in order to make an acceptable marriage, the viewpoint maintains, but women who develop eating disorders are shunned because of a strong stigma against mental illness. As a result, families often fail to report and seek help for eating disorders until the situation is almost life threatening, the Associated Press reports. There are recent efforts to address this trend.

As you read, consider the following questions:

1. Why do experts say that there is no Jewish organization that tracks the number of eating disorders among Jewish women?
2. According to a 1996 study of Jewish communities in Brooklyn, how many girls had an eating disorder?

Associated Press, "Eating Disorders Rising Problem Among Orthodox Jews," *Jerusalem Post*, December 15, 2010.

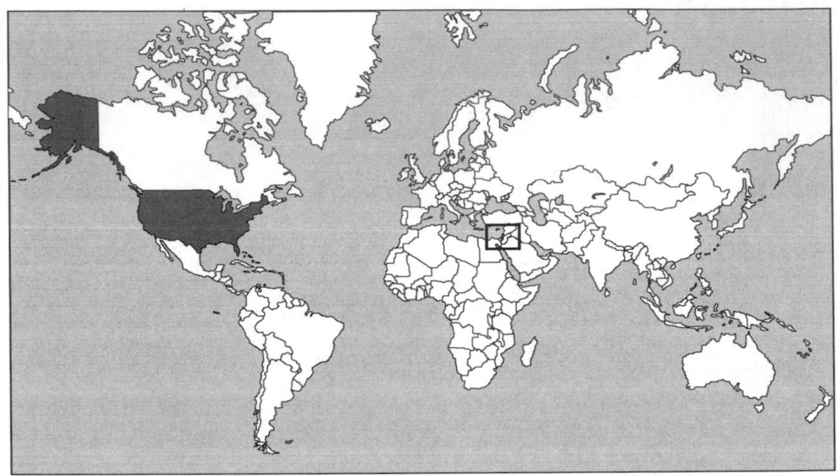

3. How many Jewish patients suffering from eating disorders did the Renfrew Center treat in 2010, according to the author?

Coconut Creek, Florida—Hilary Waller remembers begging her mother to let her fast on Yom Kippur. At 10 years old she was a bit too young, but embracing the rigid discipline seemed desperately important.

"It felt like I was practicing not eating. It was something that was reassuring and gave me strength and a sense of pride," said Waller, a 28-year-old teacher at a religious school in Blue Bell, Pennsylvania.

It was the same rush she got years later in college each time she saw the scale tip downward. Waller, who suffered from anorexia, starved herself until she stopped menstruating, lost some of her hair and was exercising several times a day.

Health experts say eating disorders are a serious, underreported disease among Orthodox Jewish women and to a lesser extent others in the Jewish community, as many families are reluctant to acknowledge the illness at all and often seek help only when a girl is on the verge of hospitalization.

Several studies indicate a rise in the problem, and those who treat eating disorders say they are seeing more Jewish patients. A new documentary, books and facilities have cropped up to help.

Waller's family, which belongs to the Conservative branch of Judaism, fasted only on Yom Kippur, but she began fasting other holidays. "And not for religious reasons," said Waller, who checked into residential treatment after college, more than a decade after she began struggling with the illness.

As eating disorders have become less taboo in mainstream US culture, they remain widely ignored in Orthodox Jewish communities, as families worry the stigma of mental illness could ruin arranged marriages for the patient and even her siblings. Strict food rituals of fasting and remaining kosher can also exacerbate the problem.

Israel has one of the highest rates of anorexia, bulimia and binge eating in the world, said Dr. Yael Latzer of the University of Haifa. No organization tracks the numbers of eating disorders among Jewish women, which experts say is partly because of a cultural reluctance to divulge the illness. Studies in different countries and Latzer's research, however, indicate a high rate in Israel.

[Eating disorders] remain widely ignored in Orthodox Jewish communities, as families worry the stigma of mental illness could ruin arranged marriages for the patient and even her siblings.

Some patients view eating disorders as a more culturally sanctioned form of rebellion in a religion where smoking and drinking are discouraged.

When Dr. Catherine Steiner-Adair arrived in Israel more than a decade ago amid pleas from Jewish activists alarmed by a spike in eating disorders, she recalls patients were so afraid to get help that they sent proxies.

"A nurse would come up to me on the street and say, 'Please help me. I'm here on behalf of a 19-year-old girl who's lost 30 pounds (13 kilograms), but she can't ask for help because she comes from a very religious family and they think it's good (for her to be underweight) because it's better for marriage making,'" said Steiner-Adair, a clinical instructor in Harvard Medical School's psychiatry department. "I was overwhelmed by the needs and the requests."

Experts say the Orthodox community is sending mixed messages to young women. Parents, matchmakers and potential mates want svelte brides, but may shun women who divulge an eating disorder because of the stigma of mental illness.

For arranged marriages among the ultra-Orthodox, the first question matchmakers ask is about physical appearance, including weight and the mother's weight, which feeds the message that thinner brides are more desirable, said Dr. Ira Sacker, who practices in New York and has written several books including *Regaining Your Self.*

In 1996, Sacker studied ultra-Orthodox and Syrian Jewish communities in Brooklyn and found that 1 out of 19 girls was diagnosed with an eating disorder, a rate about 50 percent higher than the general US population.

"It is of prime importance within the Jewish Orthodox community the bride appear to be as flawless as possible," said Rabbi Saul Zucker of the Orthodox Union, which represents Orthodox synagogues in North America.

A mental illness, such as an eating disorder "would be a terrible, terrible blemish and people will go to unbelievable lengths to hide it," he said.

Recent efforts are aiming to stop the trend. The Orthodox Union, which has been an advocate for treating drug abuse and other taboos in the Jewish community, recently released a documentary, *Hungry to Be Heard*, about the illness and started two support groups in New York City.

Eating Disorders in Israel

Israel is an important site for the study of EDs [eating disorders], particularly in relation to sociocultural aspects. This is because Israeli society encompasses various ethnic and religious groups, characterized by very old traditions on the one hand, yet being on the cutting-edge of the newest technology.

Whereas Israeli researchers have contributed significantly to the study of genetic, biological, medical, psychiatric, psychological, familial and treatment-related aspects of EDs, it is unfortunate that no systemized epidemiological studies have been conducted in Israel. Male and female Israeli adolescents have been found to be more dissatisfied with their weight and preoccupied to a greater extent with dieting and weight loss than adolescents in 34 other Western countries.

Yael Latzer, Eitan Gur, and Daniel Stein, "Editorial: Eating Disorders: Update, Controversies, and the Israeli Perspective," Israel Journal of Psychiatry and Related Sciences, *2005.*

After writing *Full of Ourselves*, which became a phenomenon among those with eating disorders, their advocates and doctors, Dr. Steiner-Adair worked with the Hadassah Foundation to write *Bishvili: For Me*, a Jewish guide to her previous book for day schools and camps.

Experts say preoccupation with food is more pronounced in the Jewish community, whether it is planning an elaborate Shabbat dinner or generally following strict kosher laws. A lot of thought goes into what is eaten and abstained from.

Kosher laws forbid eating meat and dairy at the same meal, and forbid eating pork and shellfish. Separate dishes, silverware, sinks and microwaves may also be used for meat and milk products.

"This rigidity can really be a perfect breeding ground for an eating disorder. If you're already struggling with an eating disorder and now you have all these foods that you can't eat, it can be very difficult," said Jodi Krumholz, a dietitian at the Renfrew Center, a Philadelphia-based eating disorder treatment center.

The center treated nearly 200 Jewish patients this year, up markedly from 2009.

In Jerusalem, Rabbi Shimon Herskowitz said community activists approached him about starting a small eating-disorder facility where Jewish-American parents would be comforted knowing their daughters were among staff that followed the same religious rituals. But even those parents have been reluctant.

"They only send the kids when they are totally, totally desperate, when the kid is on the borderline of hospital or residential treatment," said Herskowitz who opened Beit Chaya V'Sarah in Jerusalem last year.

Leaving treatment and reentering the tight-knit Orthodox culture also presents hurdles. For many, fasting on Yom Kippur or another holiday could cause them to relapse, but patients worry about being judged by others.

Waller felt guilty one holiday as she loaded her plate at a salad bar shortly after leaving treatment. She felt isolated from the community, unable to join in the ritual fast with the rest of her congregation, until she realized her greater sacrifice would be eating.

"For me it became the opposite. I had to give in to all the things that everyone else had been giving up," Waller said. "That was the lightbulb that reconciled the Jewish dilemma I was facing with needing to be in recovery."

Steiner-Adair says effective prevention highlights part of the religion that can inoculate girls against dangerous body messages in Western culture.

"When you have a religion that says your body is the temple of your soul and you find ways to make that meaningful at 13, that can be a very powerful way to look quite critically at Calvin Klein anorexic-chic models," she said.

VIEWPOINT 4

Middle Eastern Islamic Women Are Influenced by Western Body Images

Jason Bradley

Jason Bradley is a journalist. In the following viewpoint, he finds that eating disorders are becoming more prevalent in Middle Eastern cultures because Western ideals are being exported to Muslim countries. At one time, says Bradley, curvaceous bodies were in fashion in the Middle East; however, in recent years, the ideal body shape has gotten smaller and more in line with what is popular in Western countries. Bradley reports that experts also believe that the legacy of colonialism has profoundly influenced the changing body images in Middle Eastern cultures. One problem is the lack of treatment options for women suffering from eating disorders in the Middle East.

As you read, consider the following questions:

1. According to the author, how many college-aged American women suffer from a weight-related obsessive-compulsive disorder?
2. What percentage of American nine-year-old girls have dieted, according to Dr. Susan Ice of the Renfrew Center?

Jason Bradley, "By Barbie or Burka," *Faith Without Frontiers*, May 3, 2007. www.uiowa.edu/~c019225/barbie2.

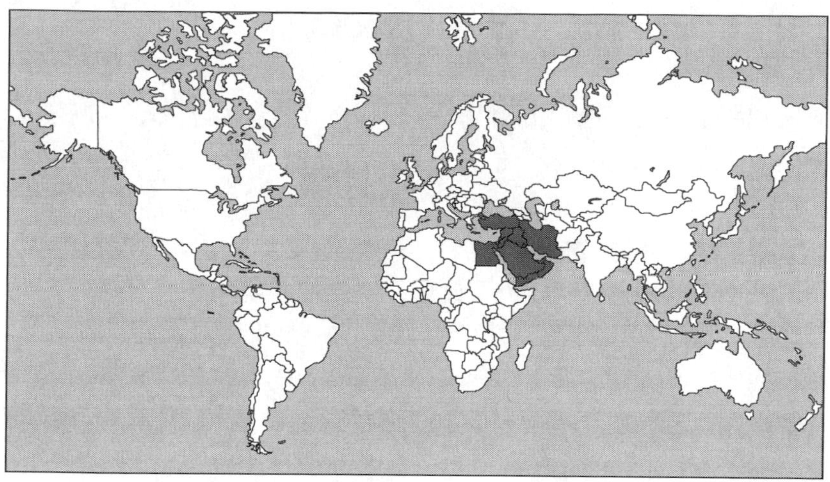

3. According to a 2004 National Institutes of Health study, how prevalent are "abnormal eating attitudes" in some specific groups in areas of Oman, Pakistan, and Turkey?

Iranian-born Yana Hamid was encouraged by her peers to starve herself. "I started fasting for Ramadan," she says, "and I just didn't quit." The majority of Muslims observe total fasting between dawn and sunset during the holy month as ordained in the Quran which says, "Fasting is prescribed to you . . . so that you may learn self-restraint."

For Yana, whose name was changed to protect her privacy, fulfilling this commandment led to unforeseen consequences.

Yana says that within the first few days of Ramadan, she began to feel better. She reports that she had more physical stamina and mental alertness. She continues, "The more I fasted, the better I felt. I felt in control. I felt closer to Allah." Her peers suggested that she was increasing her level of *iman*, or faith, and encouraged her to continue her pursuit. She adds, "I stopped eating solid foods altogether and soon I was very, very thin." Yana explains that she "felt so utterly in control—perhaps for the first time in [her] life."

But Yana continued fasting long after the holy month ended.

Eating Disorders and the Pressure to Be Thin

Like an estimated 300,000 college-aged American women, Yana Hamid suffers from a weight-related obsessive-compulsive disorder and has resorted to anorexic behaviorisms in an attempt to achieve the size-zero bodies of the models prominently displayed in the American media. But unlike most other anorexics, Yana is Middle Eastern.

Yana's parents soon became concerned and sent her to a doctor. "My first doctor actually told me that I was on a noble path and encouraged me to eat only as absolutely necessary," she says. "Eventually, I lost so much weight my parents sent me here, to the United States, for treatment." Her weight is now stabilized, but she remains concerned that she could fall "into the trap" again. Yana acknowledges that the images of women portrayed by the American media do nothing to diminish the desire to be thin, adding, "Being thin is so alluring and so accepted."

An Unattainable Image

Another young girl, 19-year-old Lebanese-American Asma Hussein, whose name was changed to protect her privacy, enjoys all the nightlife her American college town has to offer: clubs, raves, parties, pulsing beats on the dance floor, and a bounty of boys vying for her attention.

Asma plays it cool, consciously unaware of the young men as they jockey for position on the dance floor. She draws in a slow drag from her Camel Super Light.

One young gent sidles up to her and makes a pass. "You have the best eyes," he says, "and the rest is pretty fine too." He offers to buy her a drink—anything she wants. "I don't drink," she replies rejecting his advances. As the music shifts from house to a disco medley, she excuses herself from the crowd and makes her way to the restroom.

When Asma looks in the mirror she doesn't see the dark-eyed, dark-haired, olive-skinned beauty that she is told she is. Instead she sees someone that doesn't look like the women she sees in the advertisements, television shows and movies that bombard her. She would like blue eyes, lighter skin, blonde hair, and, although she weighs a mere 102 pounds, to be even thinner. She wants to be like *them*, the models she is exposed to every day.

"When I see myself, all I see is fat, fat, fat," Asma says over a cup of coffee. The coffee is the only thing she'll allow herself to eat today, or most days for that matter. Often she'll go for days without eating a single thing. "Sometimes I'll allow myself some lettuce," she says. "Or—if I'm really hungry—an apple."

A groundbreaking study . . . showed that eating disorders do indeed exist in Islamic countries, are as prevalent as in Western countries and are growing at a much faster rate.

The Rise of Eating Disorders

Worldwide, anorexia and other eating disorders are on the rise. Dr. Susan Ice, an expert in eating disorders and medical director of Philadelphia's Renfrew Center, the country's first residential facility for the treatment of women with eating disorders, finds this alarming. "The incidence of eating disorders [in America] has doubled since the 1960s and is increasing in younger age groups, in children as young as seven," she says, adding, "40 percent of [American] 9-year-old girls have dieted and even 5-year-olds are concerned about diet."

But until recently, eating disorder data did not exist in South Asian and Middle Eastern Islamic countries. Early studies indicated that eating disorders were nearly nonexistent in

Islamic countries due to the culturally ideal curvaceous female form and patriarchal social structure.

But in 2004, a groundbreaking study published by the National Institutes of Health [NIH] showed that eating disorders do indeed exist in Islamic countries, are as prevalent as in Western countries and are growing at a much faster rate. The NIH study showed "abnormal eating attitudes" to be as high as four in 10 women in some specific groups in areas of Oman, Pakistan and Turkey, a marked upswing from earlier findings. Researcher Carolyn Pedwell of the London School of Economics Gender Institute suggests that social disruption and cultural confusion have always been related to the rise in incidence of anorexia and that the recent instability in Islamic countries is no exception.

Eating Disorders Treatment in the Middle East

Despite the growing emergence of eating disorders in the Middle East, Asma says "there really are no treatment options in the Middle East—doctors generally end up putting women into psychiatric hospitals and force them to undergo electroshock therapy." Asma explains that her parents sent her to the United States so that she could get the treatment she needs without the social stigma that would come with it back in Lebanon. She says that her condition is considered "heretical" by some in her homeland, explaining that "to put yourself above your family—above god—to abuse your body like this is inexcusable."

After struggling for years in the Middle East trying to receive treatment for anorexia, Nadia Bahrami's parents also decided their best option was to find a comprehensive treatment clinic in the United States. The 20-year-old Turkish college student, whose name was changed to protect her privacy, says that she was repeatedly diagnosed as having "excessive stress," told to "take some time to relax" and that her eating habits would eventually return to normal. For Nadia and her parents, this did not seem right.

"I literally wanted to disappear," Nadia says, adding, "I was abused by my boyfriend who then left me for another girl—an American student studying abroad." She continues, "I was so jealous and did everything I could to win him back. I guess I thought that if I was very thin he would come back to me." Nadia suggests that without the availability of Western media and the portrayal of women as "waiflike sexual objects" she may not have even conceived of the idea of actually starving herself to alter her appearance. "The idea that my boyfriend would like me to be thin is one thing—but actually seeing the ads and movies . . . creates a new standard of thinness that I wouldn't have even thought about otherwise. To be a size zero became my new goal."

Nadia is now receiving counseling at the University of Iowa's eating and weight disorder program. She now weighs 123 pounds, but was a mere 94 pounds upon her arrival. She says the program, which involves weekly group counseling sessions, has allowed her to "make peace with food." Nadia says her family is very happy with her progress. She says, "They keep reminding me that being curvaceous is good—and that skinny is sick."

Changing Body Ideals in the Middle East

But the ideal of a curvaceous female form may be waning. Although some in the Muslim world consider Barbie a decadent symbol of the West—recently Saudi Arabia banned the doll along with her "revealing clothes and shameful postures"—the strikingly similar Fulla doll is taking the Muslim world by storm. Under her black head scarf and long black abaya, or robe, the Fulla doll appears to be a slightly-smaller-breasted Barbie—unattainably thin waist and all.

University of Iowa professor Meenakshi Durham, an expert in gender and body image in the media, is not surprised that American, or Western, ideals are being exported to Middle Eastern culture.

Durham explains that the legacy of colonialism has always left its mark on beauty ideals. Following slavery, lighter-skinned African-Americans were favored over darker-skinned individuals. In India and Japan, it is common to find "mixed-race" models typifying both an indigenous beauty as well as the Western ideal.

Durham says that in these colonial areas, eyelid surgeries and skin-lightening creams are commonplace in a never-ending quest to emulate the white, Western model. She notes a recent Harvard study suggesting that eating disorders did not exist in the South Pacific before Western television was available. Since then, anorexia has been on a staggering rise. "Over time, the ideal body has become slimmer, larger breasted and very muscular," she says. "That is difficult—if not impossible—to achieve by natural means."

VIEWPOINT 5

African Americans Are More Likely to Suffer from Bulimia

Cynthia Gordy

Cynthia Gordy is a journalist and blogger. In the following viewpoint, she discusses research that shows that African Americans are more likely to suffer from bulimia than white women are. Most shocking to researchers, Gordy asserts, is the evidence that it is more common for African American women to abuse laxatives or diuretics, considered a form of purging, than white women. Gordy reports that bulimic behavior is often triggered by sexual abuse and societal pressure on black women to conform to media-driven body images. Because African American women do not fit the stereotype of bulimics, they remain an underdiagnosed and undertreated community, according to Gordy. Also, many African American women suffering from the disease don't report it because of the shame of having a "white" disease.

As you read, consider the following questions:

1. According to the author, how many American women suffer from bulimia at some point in their lifetimes?
2. How much more likely than white girls are African American girls to be bulimic, according to a 2009 study?

Cynthia Gordy, "Blacks with Bulimia: A Secret in Plain Sight," *The Root*, April 28, 2011. www.theroot.com.

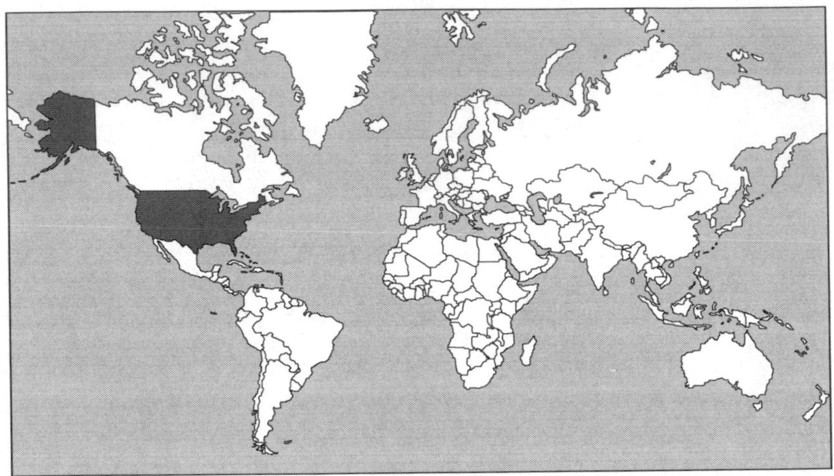

3. What percentage of people with bulimia have suffered sexual abuse, according to studies?

Debunking stereotypes, research suggests that black women are actually more likely than whites to be bulimic. So why aren't we talking about it?

Binge Eating and the Black Community

When stress mounts for Stephanie Covington Armstrong, she catches herself before reaching for comfort food. Instead she chews over what's really bothering her. "Once I can identify that, then I'm quickly able to just shift," she told the *Root*. "I've gone through a lot of therapy, so I'm very aware if I'm on the road to practicing behavior that's unhealthy."

Armstrong's mindfulness is worlds away from the years during which she responded to anxiety by binge eating, followed by hunching over the toilet to vomit, abusing laxatives or taking three consecutive aerobics classes and then doing thousands of sit-ups. Like the estimated 4.2 percent of American women who suffer from bulimia nervosa at some point in their lifetime, Armstrong was gripped by an obsessive cycle of bingeing and purging.

As a black woman, she also reflects growing research that debunks the myth that bulimia is an affluent white girl's disease—and shows that African Americans are actually *more* likely to suffer from the disorder.

A pioneering 2000 study of black women and eating disorders . . . found that black women were just as likely as white women to report recurrent binge eating and vomiting.

"Our community doesn't talk about this stuff," says Armstrong, who chronicled her battle in the 2009 memoir *Not All Black Girls Know How to Eat: A Story of Bulimia.* "I have girlfriends who've been bulimic, who casually mention it without really having any depth of conversation. Because what black woman wants to admit she can't eat? No one's tougher than us. And no one is willing to talk about it."

The Face of a Disorder

A pioneering 2000 study of black women and eating disorders, published in *Archives of Family Medicine*, found that black women were just as likely as white women to report recurrent binge eating and vomiting. It also concluded that black women are actually more likely to abuse laxatives or diuretics.

"Not much was surprising because we did this study to provide evidence that eating disorders exist in the black community, which until recently was not a widely held belief," Denise Wilfley, a lead researcher, told the *Root.* As director of the Weight Management and Eating Disorders Program at Washington University in St. Louis, Mo., which treats patients in the largely African American city, she had long known that this was the case. "But we were surprised to find that black women used more 'nontraditional' purging methods, like laxatives and diuretics." Because the public strongly associates vomiting with bulimia, Wilfley theorizes, black women may use other means without realizing that they are in fact participating in bulimic behaviors.

Surprising Research Findings

Subsequent reports have produced even more stereotype-shattering results. A 2009 study showed that not only were African American girls 50 percent more likely than white girls to be bulimic, but girls (black or white) from the lowest income bracket were also significantly more likely—153 percent more—to experience bulimia than their peers in the wealthiest group.

"We had also held the popular conception that bulimia was more common among girls from white, middle- to high-income families, so the results surprised us," Michelle Goeree, a lead researcher in the study, told the *Root*. It made more sense after the researchers realized that many insurance policies don't cover the doctor's visit where eating disorders are diagnosed, thus throwing off the documented numbers. "If two girls suffer from bulimia nervosa, but one is from a low-income family and the other from a high-income family, which girl is most likely to be diagnosed if it often requires a visit to the expensive psychiatrist?"

A 2011 study published in the *Journal of Adolescent Health* also confirms that bulimic behavior is more common among African American youths. In fact, young people from various racial backgrounds, including Asian Americans and Latinos, were found to practice extreme food-related behaviors, such as vomiting and laxative abuse, two to 10 times more often than their white counterparts.

Causes and Effects

The field of research further challenges conventional wisdom that says black women always love their curves, celebrating thickness on the strength of a community that is more accept-

The Risk of Acculturation

Since the predominant white culture has become increasingly obsessed with thinness over the last few decades, it is therefore not surprising that as a woman of color is acculturated into the mainstream, she becomes more prone to develop an eating disorder. Black females are constantly fed the message "It's bad enough that you're black, but do you have to be fat, too?" The internalization of this message can lead to low self-esteem, body dissatisfaction, and eating disorder symptomatology. With the high prevalence of obesity associated with lower socioeconomic status, it is not unexpected that black adolescent girls are developing BN [bulimia nervosa] symptomatology.

Morgan Z. Inniss, "Poor, Black, and Bulimic: A Study of Black Adolescent Females of a Lower Socioeconomic Status," VISTAS Online, *2005.*

ing of different body types. Gayle Brooks, an African American psychologist and clinical director of the Renfrew Center—an eating disorders treatment center in Coconut Creek, Fla.—says that black women feel increasingly pushed to change.

"In our society, the more you achieve and make in the world, the more you're pressured to acculturate," she told the *Root*. "Oftentimes, young African American women want to fit in, and feel they have to let go of some of the cultural norms that might have protected them in the past." Yet Brooks went on to say that it's usually not a drive for thinness at the heart of eating disorders among black women. It typically involves exposure to some type of trauma, from physical abuse to poverty, racism or a struggle with ethnic identity.

"The biggest misconception is that this is only about being thin," says Armstrong, noting that most people with bulimia are either a normal weight or slightly overweight. "I don't believe that's the first reason. It comes from some kind of trauma and a need for control—you don't just wake up one day and decide to throw up."

In Armstrong's case, the trigger was being raped by an uncle when she was 12. Having grown up in a fatherless Brooklyn, N.Y., household, she says that being assaulted by her single male role model left her feeling worthless. "I had no other men in my life who loved me to help me see, 'This person is messed up.' For me it became, 'I'm messed up.'" Studies show that roughly 60 percent of people with bulimia have suffered sexual abuse.

A Harmful Coping Mechanism

Armstrong turned to bingeing and purging as a coping mechanism for her anxiety and low self-esteem after getting the idea from a magazine article intended as a cautionary tale for teens. Laxative abuse and excessive exercise soon followed. "At the height of it, I was throwing up eight to 10 times a day. Afterward, there would be this calm," says Armstrong, now in her 40s. "I could not control the external circumstances of my life, but I could control my relationship to food."

Meanwhile, her family and friends never connected the dots. Watching her inhale large quantities of food, they just marveled at her ability to stay skinny. "It was like they were envious, which only fueled a feeling of superiority," she said. After living with her secret for seven years—so obsessed, depressed and suicidal that she could barely function—she finally sought help and checked into a 12-step program. "I was desperate around food, and at a certain point I just couldn't live like that anymore."

A Secret Shame

Despite the research indicating that bulimia occurs disproportionately among African American women, stories like Armstrong's are virtually invisible in both the study and treatment of eating disorders and in the black community. Brooks explains that, because black women don't fit the presumed profile, education efforts have not been directed at them, causing family and friends to miss warning signs. Furthermore, many doctors and therapists fail to make proper assessments.

"Doctors tend to not recognize it in African American women, so they don't make appropriate referrals for treatment," Brooks says, adding that studies have shown that it takes longer for black girls to be diagnosed with eating disorders than it does white girls who have the same symptoms.

There's also the matter of black women hiding bulimia because they think it's a "white" disease. "This attitude may lead black women to experience a double layer of shame—shame because eating disorders are seen as the result of vanity run amok, and shame because it may be viewed as a betrayal of their cultural roots," says Wilfley. "The issue may also go back to a general reluctance on the part of many members of the black community to recognize mental illness and seek help."

A Code of Silence

Armstrong agrees that there is a "code of silence" around mental health disorders. "Whenever we have an experience that makes us fall outside of the Strong Black Woman archetype, we go quiet," she says. "We assume that as black women, we can handle our whole lives. If someone goes to therapy, many of us assume they're crazy. If you need help, we think there's something wrong with you."

Today Armstrong, a married mother living in Los Angeles, works with the National Eating Disorders Association's Diversity Task Force and speaks at colleges, high schools and organizations to help raise awareness. "I'm recovered now and don't struggle at all," she says. But in her outreach, she has met hundreds of African American girls and women still suffering in the shadows. "I would just love to see people get the help they need, without the fear of judgment and the isolation. It's time to talk about it."

Periodical and Internet Sources Bibliography

The following articles have been selected to supplement the diverse views presented in this chapter.

Adriana Barton	"Are Middle-Aged Women Succumbing to 'Desperate Housewives Syndrome?'" *Globe and Mail* (Canada), May 1, 2011.
Samantha Brett	"Does Porn Culture Distort Our Body Image?," *Sydney Morning Herald*, December 13, 2011.
Matt Chorley	"Quick-Fix Diets Drive Teens to Hate Their Bodies," *Independent* (London), November 27, 2011.
Roscoe Elliott	"Body Image Differs in Brazil," *Daily Bruin* (UCLA), February 16, 2010.
David Graham	"Boys Don't Want to Be 'Buff'," *Toronto Star*, October 3, 2011.
Vivien Hoexter	"From Generation to Generation: How Not to Visit Our Body Image Sins on Our Children," *Huffington Post*, December 2, 2011. www.huffingtonpost.com.
Alok Jha	"Distorted Body Image Means People Don't Know the Back of Their Own Hands," *Guardian* (UK), June 14, 2010.
Robin Knowles	"Rise in Men Suffering from Eating Disorders, Say GPs," BBC News, July 13, 2011. www.bbc.co.uk.
Tsafi Saar	"Image Wars," *Haaretz* (Israel), May 25, 2010.
Mary Sanchez	"For Healthier Female Body Images, Let's Drop Photoshop," *Kansas City Star*, December 8, 2011.

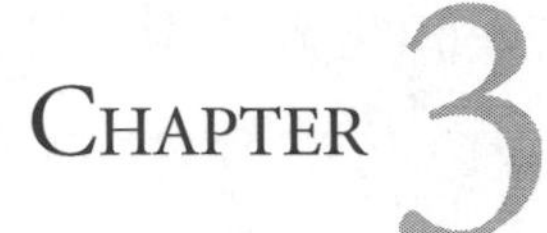

The Relationship Between the Media and Eating Disorders

VIEWPOINT 1

The Global Problem of Eating Disorders Is Fueled by the Media

Dana Lonergan, John Arcarola, Amanda Kern, and Renee Daniel

Dana Lonergan, John Arcarola, Amanda Kern, and Renee Daniel are contributors to the PT Companion. In the following viewpoint, they examine the global problem of eating disorders and contend that much of the blame for the rising epidemic around the world can be placed on the media, which broadcast and perpetuate Western ideals of beauty. The authors suggest that the media trigger the disease in men and women who are vulnerable and already feel pressured to reach and maintain an unrealistic and unhealthy body image. Although the media have fueled the rise of the disease, the authors assert there is an opportunity for the media to help combat it in the future by providing healthier and more realistic body images for the public.

As you read, consider the following questions:

1. According to the authors, how many Americans have an eating disorder?
2. How many people worldwide do the authors estimate have an eating disorder?

3. What is Dove's "Real Beauty" campaign?

Eating disorders are becoming an extremely common problem among young adolescents. From both a national and global standpoint, societies are experiencing a rise in the prevalence of this epidemic. The influence of the media is largely to blame for this concerning issue. In everyday society, we are bombarded with commercials, magazines, radio, music, newspapers, movies, and music videos that portray the socially ideal body. Adolescents, especially, often experience a great deal of pressure from these unrealistic examples of beauty and feel as if they must be thin to be considered beautiful through the eyes of their peers, family, and society. It is from these constant pressures that eating disorders commonly develop and endanger the health of adolescents worldwide. Body image is defined as the mental representation of one's physical self at any given point in time. Throughout the world, the media has made an enormous impact on how people interpret their own body image, as well as that of others.

The Dangers of Eating Disorders

Among the different variations of eating disorders, anorexia nervosa and bulimia nervosa are the most widespread and commonly diagnosed. The development of each is strongly correlated with earlier upbringings, such as an unstable home life or dysfunctional relationships. The most concerning problem with these eating disorders is that they tend to be difficult to identify until most of the damage to the body has already been done. At first, signs of eating disorders in some adolescents can be hard to detect from physical outward appearance, and commonly remain undetected until evidence of serious health issues arise. For doctors, diagnosing an eating disorder can be extremely difficult due to the fact that many young girls and boys do not wish to speak about their health and eating habits.

Anorexia nervosa is an eating disorder in which the individual does not eat enough calories per day to sustain a normal, healthy weight, or receive proper vitamins and nutrients. Individuals with anorexia will not immediately show outward signs of the disease, mainly due to the fact that initially, the body is depleting the storage of nutrients found in muscles and bones. However, very quickly after those storage sites are depleted, the overall health of the person is apparent. The body becomes extremely gaunt and frail, and the skin bruises easily—lanugo hair may develop as a mechanism for insulation, due to the body's response to the loss of body fat. Finally, even more concerning physical effects include the loss of a menstrual period in women, decreased heart rate, iron deficiency, and low blood potassium.

For doctors, diagnosing an eating disorder can be extremely difficult due to the fact that many young girls and boys do not wish to speak about their health and eating habits.

Bulimia nervosa, on the other hand, is when an individual engages in cycles of food binging and purging, usually by vomiting, or the misuse of laxatives. Psychologically, those with bulimia believe that purging will immediately get rid of the excess calories that they just ate. However, in reality, calorie absorption begins almost immediately. People with bulimic behavior are rarely diagnosed because the outward physical signs are not quite as apparent as in anorexia nervosa. Serious health risks with bulimia include rotting of the teeth from constant vomiting, stomach ulcers, and low blood potassium.

The Prevalence of Eating Disorders

These eating disorders can develop in both men and women. Usually, the disorders are most common during the teen years. During these years, peer pressure plays a major role in how a person views him or herself. Nonetheless, eating disorders also affect older adults or even young preteens. Most eating disorders occur due to extreme lack of self-esteem, peer pressure, depression, unstable home life, and most significantly, the media. Young adolescents are at an extremely vulnerable stage in which the ideas and opinions of others tend to rank higher than their own individual ideas.

The Influence of the Media

The media focuses its attention specifically on this age group in hopes to use beauty and sex to sell products. The media creates a category of beauty that sets a standard for adolescents to live up to. The media created the image that "thin is beautiful," or "thin is in." These portrayals of models with a low body weight psychologically affect the minds of adolescents and lead them to believe that a healthy body weight is actually fat. But in reality, the body weight that society says is beautiful is much lower than the body weight of a normal adolescent going through puberty. Among the several other contributing factors of this global issue, such as dysfunctional family life, low self-esteem, and depression, influence from popular culture portrayed in the media seems to be the most commonly associated psychological trigger for the development of eating disorders. Some studies even suggest that the media is an actual causal risk factor for eating disorders instead of a strong influence.

The true causes of eating disorders are unknown. The United States, specifically, has a social and cultural ideal of extreme thinness. Women, in particular, define themselves by how physically attractive they are and often resort to extreme measures to achieve beauty. Throughout the United States, eating disorders are rapidly becoming a common issue in modern society. The media has a major influence on the development of eating disorders. It helps to set unrealistic expectations on what body image is considered beautiful. Adolescents are constantly exposed to critical body image tabloids and American magazines such as *Cosmopolitan* that reinforce the idea that to be happy and successful, they must be thin. The idea of obtaining "perfection," is seen through an image and therefore, gives an individual with an eating disorder an image to become.

The most recent statistics in the United States relating to eating disorders are disturbing; they show that no gender, race, social class or culture is immune to the disease. Thousands of teenage girls are starving themselves this very minute trying to attain what the fashion industry considers to be the "ideal" figure. The average Victoria's Secret model weighs 23% less than the average American woman. By maintaining a weight that is 15% below your expected body weight, one fits the credentials for anorexia. Consequently, most models, according to medical standards, fit into the category of being anorexic. Teenagers need to realize that society's ideal body image is not achievable. In addition, the photos we see in magazines are not real either. Teens striving to attain society's unattainable ideal image will ultimately end up increasing their feelings of inadequacy. Teenagers are under a lot of pressure to be thin; they are led to believe that the only way they can be accepted and fit in, is if they are thin. With that, they resort to starving, vomiting, and eating only diet foods.

Startling Statistics

In the United States, it is estimated that eight million Americans have an eating disorder, consisting of seven million women and one million men. An estimated 10–15% of people with anorexia or bulimia are males. Nearly half of all Americans personally know someone with an eating disorder. Eating disorders have the highest mortality rate out of any existing mental illness. The mortality rate associated with nervosa is twelve times higher than the death rate or all causes of death for females 15–24 years old. A study by the National Association of Anorexia Nervosa and Associated Disorders reported that 5–10% of anorexics die within ten years after contracting the disease; 18–20% of anorexics will be dead after twenty years, and only 30–40% ever fully recover. After suffering from anorexia, 20% of people will prematurely die from complications related to their eating disorder, including suicide and heart problems.

Only one in ten people with eating disorders receive treatment. About 80% of women who have accessed care for their eating disorders, do not get the intensity of treatment they need to stay in recovery; they are often sent home weeks earlier than the recommended stay. Treatment of an eating disorder in the U.S. ranges from $500 to $2,000 per day. The average cost for a month of inpatient treatment is $30,000. It is estimated that individuals with eating disorders need anywhere from three to six months of inpatient care.

A Global Disease

Eating disorders are not just a major problem in the United States, but exist among societies all over the world as well. Approximately 70 million people worldwide struggle with eating disorders, with the highest prevalence unsurprisingly, being among countries of Western culture, including Canada, New Zealand, Australia, Europe, and South Africa. The sociocultural attitudes of these societies, which are highly influenced by the unrealistic examples portrayed in the media, put individuals, especially women, with predisposed psychological tendencies towards eating disorders at great risk. Thinness is highly emphasized as an essential aspect of attractiveness throughout the media, while at the same time, these airbrushed and Photoshopped models are being used to advertise the abundance of unhealthy food consumption and sedentary living. In general, people who develop eating disorders have low self-esteem and are very susceptible to societal influ-

Can We Be Certain That the Media Must Share the Blame?

A stark example of the media's overwhelming influence was seen in Fiji as the introduction of television led to a radical outbreak of eating disorders. Traditionally, Fiji's culture esteemed a fuller figure and was relatively free of any insecurity about body image. In 1995, a television channel from Western culture featuring shows like *Seinfeld, ER, Melrose Place* and *Xena: Warrior Princess*, was introduced in Fiji. Within just thirty-eight months, a survey reported 74% of Fujian teenage girls [had] negative feelings about their body image. Among these girls, there was a sharp increase in characteristics of eating disorders, with about 15% of them admitting to bulimic behaviors. This rapid transformation within this innocent culture represents the severity of the media's control and the dangers associated with its growing influence.

Dana Lonergan, John Arcarola,
Amanda Kern, and Renee Daniel,
"Eating Disorders and Popular Culture from a Global and National Standpoint," PT Companion,
December 7, 2010. http://theptcompanion.com.

ences. The media does not directly cause these problems, but definitely influences the way people feel about themselves.

Throughout history, larger figures were desirable and were strongly correlated with high social class and wealth, due to an abundance of food and life of luxury. Now, with modernization and development of the Western world, this viewpoint has dramatically shifted, deeming excess weight an unattractive and even shameful attribute. As recent globalization of non-Western cultures has become increasingly prevalent, areas of the world undergoing these different societal changes are becoming particularly at risk for developing symptoms of eating disorders. Increased media exposure of Western cultures in many areas, such as the Middle East and Asia, has placed societal pressures upon these cultures to conform to Western standards. High rates of dieting, especially among women, have become present in these cultures in efforts to mimic the typical, yet unrealistic, images portrayed in Western media. Self-conscious attitudes about body image were also highly increased in these areas.

This trend is also seen among non-Western immigrant populations in Western societies. Many individuals who move to Western cultures strive for acceptance and typically attempt to learn about societal norms through the media. Again, they are highly susceptible to these influences and commonly will make drastic changes to fit in, which very often leads to disordered eating. To investigate the possibility of increased eating disorders associated with exposure to Western culture, two female Arabic populations, one in a Cairo university and one in a London university, were studied. While no cases of eating disorders were found in the Cairo group, a shocking twelve percent of the London group reported to have bulimia nervosa, which is the highest rate ever reported among a group of women living in England.

As recent globalization of non-Western cultures has become increasingly prevalent, areas of the world undergoing these different societal changes are becoming particularly at risk for developing symptoms of eating disorders.

The Challenges of Recovery

The media's influence on the development of eating disorders is vast, and the battle towards recovery can be an overwhelming, seemingly impossible challenge for many individuals with this disease. Anorexia and bulimia are severe mental illnesses that, over time, can completely take over all aspects of one's life. The original triggers, such as a desire to be thin or accepted, soon become an afterthought for some, as the disease becomes an obsession, grasping hold of the mind, body, and spirit like an addicting drug. A website, called Pro-Ana Nation, describes the disturbing reality of a woman's battle with a combination of anorexia and bulimia. The website provides information about the several underlying mental health conditions which are often seen with eating disorders as well as statistical information about the dangers of these diseases. However, even though this woman is aware of all this information, she proceeds to describe her overwhelming battle with the disease and discusses her obsession with continuing to live that way. The disease has caused her to live in almost complete isolation, and has taken control of her priorities. "I hate my eating disorder as much as I need it. It has become a part of my identity, and distracts me from serious, emotional issues in my life," she states.

How the Media Can Combat the Problem

Because the media has such great control over individuals, especially those with predisposed conditions, many efforts to combat the problem are beginning to appear in the popular media. In 2004, Dove launched the "Real Beauty" campaign, with advertisements featuring the average, real woman, comfortable with her larger body and shape. . . .

All around the world, there are physicians and medical clinics that work with people every day to help cure the negative effects of eating disorders. However, it is not often that you see commercials on television, or advertisements on the radio, expressing where to go to seek help for these personal, private problems. On the contrary, the Internet, a source of media, changes all of that. The Internet, to most, is a place where they can truly express how they feel and talk about their problems, without anyone ever knowing who they are. This is often seen in blogs and online support groups.

Nationally, and globally, people are accessing these websites looking for an answer to their eating disorder. One website, called EatingDisordersOnline.com, is an immense website that provides easy routes to several directions that one can go. For example, this website contains several links to exterior websites of doctors and clinics that they can contact. Also, the website provides an endless amount of information on all forms of eating disorders, and how they do harm to one's body. In addition, the most common on this website is the link titled "Support Groups." When someone connects to that link, there are hundreds of blogs and fellow people who share the same problems. These blogs provide a setting where people can relate to others, and they work together to try to get over their problems. Conquering the mind of one's self is a hard task. The media has done a tremendous job at promoting that skinny, fit, and beautiful is the way to be accepted in society.

Because the media has such great control over individuals, especially those with predisposed conditions, many efforts to combat the problem are beginning to appear in the popular media.

Finding the Root Causes of Eating Disorders

Another frequently visited online worldwide website is one called Something-Fishy.org. The Something Fishy mission statement states, "we are dedicated to raising awareness about eating disorders . . . emphasizing always that eating disorders are *not* about food and weight; they are just the symptoms of something deeper going on, inside. Something Fishy is determined to remind each and every sufferer of anorexia, bulimia, compulsive overeating and binge eating disorder that they are not alone, and that complete recovery is possible." Here, this form of media is providing privacy, comfort, support, and a way out. The media is not all bad; there are still forms of media, such as these websites, that are trying to reach out to those who suffer from eating disorders, to help them.

From a global standpoint, eating disorders still remain a problem. On a daily basis, body image is portrayed in the media, and it will continue to be that way for a long time. As we have seen, the media can have a negative effect on how one views their own body image, leading to eating disorders. Can this ever be completely changed? We see how there are forms of media advertisements that reach out to those in need of help from the detriments of eating disorders; can those few media approaches overpower the ideal body image? Only time will tell, but the controversy of the media influencing the prevalence of eating disorders is a topic that will remain [of] interest to the public.

VIEWPOINT 2

Weighing Up a Media Culture That Sees 58-cm Waistlines as the Norm

Philip Brasor

Philip Brasor is a reporter for the Japan Times. *In the following viewpoint, he discusses the high rate of eating disorders in Japan, an epidemic that he feels is exacerbated by media that treat extreme thinness as the norm. In many cases, Brasor believes that the Japanese media's emphasis on unrealistic body images has muted recognition of the problem and has hindered attempts to deal with it. In Japan, many women are obsessed with maintaining tiny waistlines, a trend set by Japanese celebrities. According to Brasor, it seems that these attitudes are impervious to ridicule and reason.*

As you read, consider the following questions:

1. What is the optimum waistline measurement desired by women in Japan, according to the magazine *Aera*?
2. According to the Japanese health ministry, how much has the average weight of Japanese women in their thirties decreased over the past twenty years?
3. What percentage of Japanese women between the ages of twenty and forty are underweight?

Philip Brasor, "Weighing Up a Media Culture That Sees 58-cm Waistlines as the Norm," *The Japan Times*, April 27, 2008. www.japantimes.co.jp.

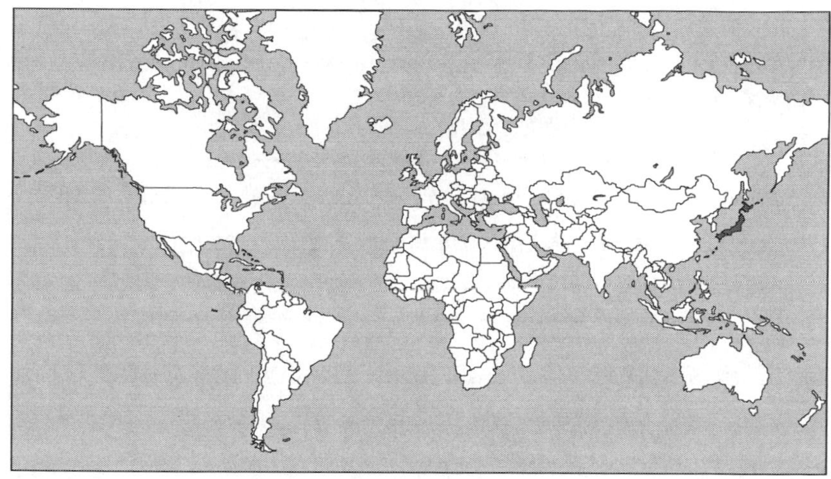

Earlier this month, the French Parliament began contemplating a bill that would make it illegal to promote extreme thinness. Following the death in 2006 of a Brazilian supermodel from complications associated with anorexia, the issue of young women purposely starving themselves for the sake of self-image has come to be taken very seriously, and not just in the fashion world.

Eating disorders like anorexia and bulimia are not unknown in Japan, but their recognition is muted by a media culture that takes extreme thinness for granted. An article in last week's issue of *Aera* says the quest for the smallest waistline is not confined to teens and young women, the demographic most associated with extreme thinness.

The article focuses on a 48-year-old homemaker named Shino, whose own abdomen is an astonishingly tight 56 cm. Shino used to fluctuate between 63 and 66 cm until she gave birth, after which she ballooned to 86 cm. She was so depressed that she became a recluse and even thought about suicide. None of the dieting methods she tried worked, and then one day, while taking in the laundry, she came up with an odd but apparently effective exercise method while taking in the washing. Within six months she was back to her old waist size and just kept going, parlaying her success with weight loss into success as a fitness guru. Her books have sold more than 900,000 copies.

Eating disorders like anorexia and bulimia are not unknown in Japan, but their recognition is muted by a media culture that takes extreme thinness for granted.

Shino's waist is extreme even by current standards of skinny. According to *Aera*, the waistline measurement that's optimally desired by women in Japan is 58 cm (which, coincidentally or not, is the numerical inversion of 85 cm, the waist size experts cite as a prime indicator of metabolic syndrome in men).

However, 58 isn't an arbitrary number. Linguist Asako Iida says in the article that the number has a strong "subliminal effect." In 2001, undergarment maker Wacoal polled women who felt the ideal waist size was 60 cm. Iida says that women tended to "reduce" their measurements. Moreover, "8" has significance in Japanese numerology, as evidenced by the practice of ending retail prices with an 8 or an 8 followed by a zero. In America, stores will set a price at $9.99 because it seems cheaper than $10.00. In Japan, using a "9" is considered too obvious a sales ploy, so "8" is used instead. Japanese women use the same line of reasoning in terms of their figures.

The 58-cm target goes back to the 1970s when pinup idols like Agnes Lam and Masako Natsume "publicly announced" that they had 58-cm waistlines. *Aera* implies that these measurements were probably not true, but in any case the number took root as the ideal for female celebrities whose careers are based on their looks—pretty much all of them.

The article includes a chart listing the "official" measurements of some of Japan's most popular female celebrities, and no one has a waistline larger than 60 cm. A Wacoal publicist

Japan's "Culture of Cute"

Whereas thinness in Western conceptualization is often associated with providing power and control that will, in turn, convey happiness, the Japanese pursuit of thinness is more reminiscent . . . of eating disorders as a strategy for delaying maturation and the pursuant responsibilities. As described in . . . case histories, thinness was not associated with expanding one's sense of power or competence. Instead, in these case examples the pursuit of thinness was subjectively experienced as an attempt to rejoin one's peer group from an earlier time and resist the demands associated with mature adult relationships. Clearly this dynamic is not unique to eating disorders in Japan; however, it has particular heuristic value in understanding the contemporary Japanese cultural context.

Kathleen M. Pike and Amy Borovoy,
"The Rise of Eating Disorders in Japan: Issues of Culture and Limitations of the Model of 'Westernization,'"
Culture, Medicine and Psychiatry, *December 2004.*

says that people in her industry take these claims with a grain of salt. She assumes they're probably closer to around 67 cm, which is still slim. Wacoal's research has found that compared to women in other world capitals, women in Tokyo have higher bust-to-waist and hips-to-waist ratios, meaning their proportions (merihari) are considered more pleasing to the eye. However, the same research found that more women in Tokyo are dissatisfied with their bodies than Parisian women, whose merihari ratios happen to be much lower than their Tokyo counterparts.

The reality is approaching the ideal. According to the health ministry, the average weight of Japanese women in their 30s has decreased by about 12 percent over the last 20 years, and 20 percent of all women between the ages of 20 and 40 are, medically speaking, underweight. The ministry even says that women are, on average, lighter now than they were right after the war, when a lot of Japanese people couldn't eat.

This trend is a media creation. Many advertising campaigns feature females who are very skinny and, depending on the product, anxious about their figures.

In a commercial for Suntory's Oolong Tea, a Chinese ballet dancer advises another dancer who is not eating to drink the beverage with her meals if she's worried about getting fat. Laxatives are aimed exclusively at women, indirectly marketed as diet aids. Many bulimics use them religiously, so it's a little unsettling to see the commercial for Biofermin's new laxative for children in which a 12-year-old girl yells happily to her mother "Deta! (It came out!)."

These commercials would have no purchase on viewer imaginations if it weren't for a media culture that sees women with (allegedly) 58-cm waistlines as the norm. All other women on TV are rendered as being abnormal. Full-figured TV personalities are classified as *debu tarento* (fat talent) with no identity separate from their body image.

Comedian Kanako Yanagihara takes advantage of her unfashionable proportions in her routines, many of which lampoon the vacuousness of girl-centered consumer culture. People laugh, but as shown on a segment of the now defunct Fuji TV variety show *Saturday Midnight Channel*, these attitudes are impervious to ridicule.

In that segment, Yanagihara tried out for a job at Cecil McBee's in Shibuya 109, Japan's youth fashion mecca, whose sales clerks are as famous as magazine models. The store manager complimented Yanagihara's people skills, but the staff are required to wear the clothes they sell, and there was nothing in Yanagihara's size, which is XL.

It's not just Cecil McBee's. Go to almost any non-specialty clothing store in Japan and you will have a hard time finding women's clothes marked as any size larger than M. That's because retailers believe no woman will buy anything marked L, much less XL. It's as if normal bodies didn't exist anymore.

VIEWPOINT 3

Women in the United Arab Emirates Are Being Pressured by Western Media to Develop Eating Disorders

Rania Moussly

Rania Moussly is a staff reporter for Gulf News. *In the following viewpoint, she investigates the findings of a recent study in the United Arab Emirates (UAE) on the effects of the media on Emirati women's perceptions of body image. According to Moussly, the research shows that an alarming number of female college students show signs of having an eating disorder and are affected by the depiction of unrealistic body images in the media. Many of these distorted body images are coming from the Western media. Eating disorders in the UAE are particularly hard to diagnose and treat, and the study shows that there needs to be more treatment options for women and men suffering from these disorders in the UAE.*

As you read, consider the following questions:

1. According to a recent study of female college students in the UAE, how many of them can be classified as possibly having an eating disorder?

Rania Moussly, "Falling Prey to Eating Disorders: A Study Suggests Women Students in the UAE Are Heavily Influenced by the Media and the Pressure to Look Good," *Gulf News*, May 23, 2010. gulfnews.com.

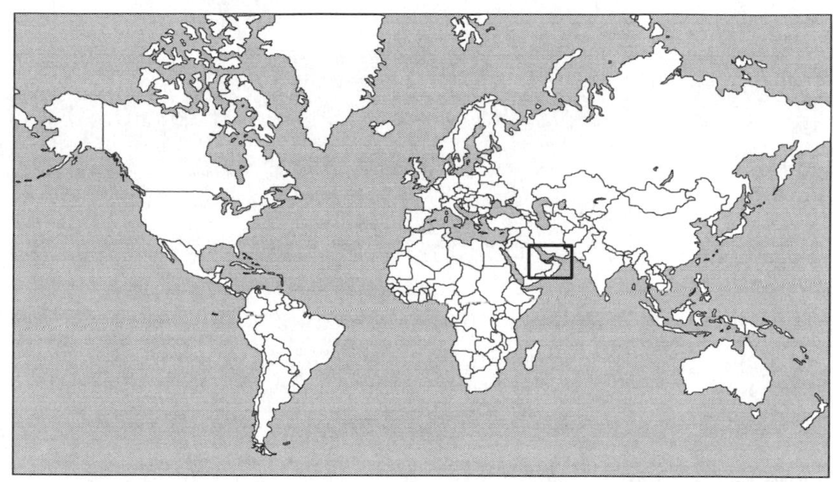

2. What percentage of Emirati college women surveyed watched at least seventeen hours of television a week, according to the study?
3. How much more common are eating disorders in Emirati women than men, according to the study?

A recent survey of nearly 500 women Emirati university students showed a quarter of them fell in the category of possibly having eating disorders.

A Groundbreaking Study

Amani Al Hashemi, a student counsellor at the Abu Dhabi Women's College (ADWC), who will soon publish the findings of her study, is investigating the effects of the media on Emirati women's body image and self-perception.

The study is a collaboration with Dr Justin Thomas, assistant professor of clinical psychology at Zayed University. The paper, "Eating Attitudes and Body Image Concerns Among Female University Students in the United Arab Emirates," is set to be published in *Appetite*, an international research journal specialising in behavioural nutrition.

Research Results

The investigation showed young women in the UAE [United Arab Emirates] need to be aware of the distorted, unrealistic representation of women's bodies in the media.

"The findings show a need to establish clinics and increase services for women who already suffer from eating disorders," said Amani.

"Especially with news stories reporting about Emirati families having to travel abroad to seek help for their daughters," she added.

"We focused on the university population because they are a high-risk group," said Thomas.

"If someone is going to develop an eating disorder, that is the mostly likely age they will do it at," he added.

The Role of the Media

Amani's study shows that increased media influence and repeated exposure to a "distorted image of reality" played a significant role in the rising increase of inclinations to developing eating disorders amongst young Emirati women.

"This distortion is manifested in many ways, some of which are the over-representation of underweight ultra-thin models," said Amani.

Almost 90 per cent of students used in her sample reported watching at least 17 hours of television a week, while nearly 75 per cent reported reading appearance-related magazines, indicating that repeated exposure is a factor.

"Some studies I have researched say women are affected by the media they watch. With repeated exposure to the thin ideal, it makes them start to accept the models shown as a true representation of reality," said Amani.

The Pervasiveness of Western Media

"Various sources show that when Western media becomes a significant influence in non-Western cultures there are significant changes in all sorts of ways," said Annie Crookes, senior lecturer of psychology at Middlesex University Dubai.

"Things such as fast-food eateries were never around before as they are not traditional in certain cultures, but instead [they are] an idea introduced somewhat by the media," she added.

"I think it's also an issue of control and anxiety during such a transitional phase in their life. The way to gain some control over their life is through what they are eating, as it helps them delay the anxiety," said Crookes.

Feeling the Pressure

Increased symptoms of eating disorders in the UAE are not limited to Emirati female students as women of all nationalities feel pressured to look good. Eating disorders are also common in some men, but according to Amani's research they are ten times more prevalent in women.

"There is an appearance standard the media sets which has a certain affect on even guys but I don't think it's as extreme for us as it is for women," said Sawan Kotecha, business student from Middlesex University Dubai.

Increased symptoms of eating disorders in the UAE are not limited to Emirati female students as women of all nationalities feel pressured to look good.

"There are many desirable types of bodies a guy can have, but for girls it's mostly the slim and slender look."

He went on to say that although there is an impact of the media on men in relation to their body image and self-esteem, it does not show it much.

"Guys don't discuss it with each other, but there is definitely a mental effect," said Kotecha.

The Pressure to Look Good

For women it is the complete opposite.

"It [body image and they way we look] is something we always talk about," said Yasmine Nagm, mass communications and psychology student at the American University of Sharjah.

"Whenever we make plans, especially with summer coming up, we are always talking about fixing our bodies and looking good."

Yasmine said the urgency to look good comes from external influences.

"I feel pressured to look good because there is a standard for how the body should look and the standard we expect is not what we are getting."

Yasmine added that the standard for her and her peers is set by models and celebrities who have specific sizes.

An Underreported and Undertreated Disease

"Eating disorders are a problem, a very big problem even though they go undiagnosed," said Fadwa Lkorchy, student counsellor, Sharjah Women's College.

"The students don't come for help, we usually pick them up if they are fainting in college or having trouble concentrating in class, or by their physical appearance," she added. She said most of the girls don't recognise it as a problem because of their obsession with looking perfect.

"Nowadays eating disorders can easily be masked by fashion, because everyone is thin now, that is the trend."

She said some student diets consist solely of fizzy drinks and crisps.

The Role of Globalisation

"Globalisation is affecting everybody. In the Arab Muslim world, we take everything and anything without critical evaluation of what will fit our culture and what will not," Fadwa said.

© Danesh Mohiuddin/Xpress

"This is an interesting yet dangerous topic which needs to be addressed, but we can't do that until we get the numbers and have a significant number of people identified [as having] eating disorders," she added.

"Advertisements showing wafer-thin models send an implicit message to the public to starve themselves; but then, she is eating a burger. So the explicit message is to also consume," said Thomas.

"Such messages embed an idea that you are supposed to be able to eat those things and still be able to stay skinny," said Crookes.

"That is very anxiety-driving because people start to think 'well what's wrong with me? Why can't I do that?' It makes them feel like a failure when they eat that kind of food [and] don't get the same results. It can be unstable as a psychological message," she added.

Viewpoint 4

China Blames the West and Western Media for an Increase in Eating Disorders

Stina Björkell

Stina Björkell is a contributing writer to Radio86.com. In the following viewpoint, she explores the rising rates of eating disorders in China, reporting that China's increasing affluence has led to a prevalence of Western self-obsession and distorted views of self in the country. Unfortunately, she asserts, there is a stigma in China attached to mental illness that hinders many women and men from seeking treatment. Chinese media need to work harder to raise awareness of this growing trend, Björkell argues.

As you read, consider the following questions:

1. Where does the author say that most of the Chinese people suffering from eating disorders live?
2. According to the author, what do some of the more dangerous diet pills contain?
3. How does the author say that the Chinese mentality changed in the past ten years?

Eating disorders such as anorexia nervosa and bulimia nervosa used to be considered lifestyle diseases of people in the rich countries of the West, who lead a life of ease and want for nothing. Recently, however, there has been an alarm-

Stina Björkell, "Eating Disorders in China: A Sign of the Times," Radio86.com, February 15, 2011. radio86.com.

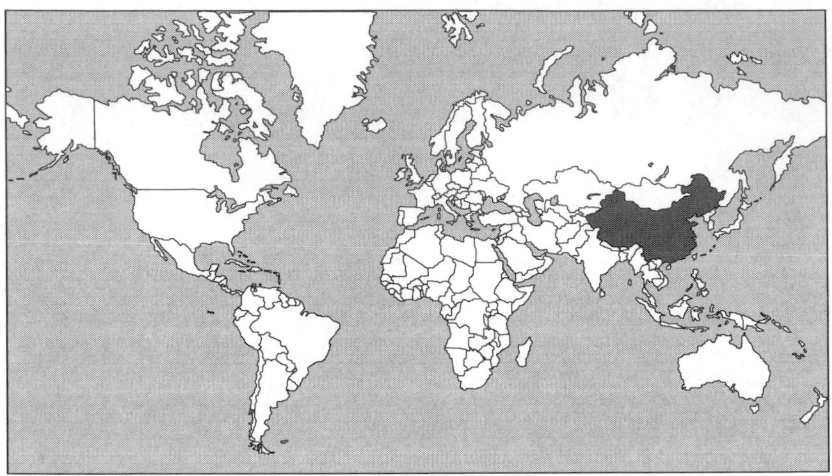

ing increase in such disorders in China, which is still officially a developing country. Surprising? Maybe not, considering that most of the people suffering from these afflictions live in China's burgeoning coastal metropolises where most of the country's money is located. So, the generalization that can be made from this is that—wherever people live in the lap of luxury, there you will also find those who are battling eating disorders.

The underlying causes of eating disorders and their patterns of occurrence follow a common path all over the world. For example, just like in the West, only a fraction of Chinese patients suffering from these dangerous conditions are male. In addition, most of the patients with anorexia come from rich families, which excludes malnutrition as a cause.

One of the biggest, and most dangerous, eating disorders is anorexia, where patients can go for days without eating or eating only very minute amounts, starving themselves, sometimes to the point of death. In one, more easily hidden, form of anorexia, patients not only starve themselves, but also purge by vomiting or taking laxatives. If both binge eating and purging occur on a regular basis, the disorder is usually diagnosed as bulimia nervosa.

As for the telltale signs of eating disorders, they can be difficult to spot as patients usually try to hide their compulsions. However, excessive exercising is one of the most conspicuous signs of bulimia and anorexia, both of which are mainly triggered by social pressures. More often than not, eating disorders are brought on by an uncontrollable obsession with one's physical appearance and the need to feel attractive and popular.

Undiscriminating Lifestyle Diseases

Numerous studies on the subject of eating disorders have found that they affect all kinds of people regardless of gender, age, race, class or sexual preference. However, there are some common denominators to be found among patients, including a relatively comfortable lifestyle in an urban environment, a good education and the female gender.

Thus, treatment centers for people with eating disorders are appearing all over the world, even in the Middle East, Africa and Asia. And what is very concerning is that in China, in particular, the incidence of anorexia has risen sharply in recent years.

One factor which often delays the diagnosis and treatment of eating disorders in China is that there is still a strong stigma attached to mental illnesses, which means that many people postpone going to the doctor for as long as possible. In addition, many doctors are still not trained to spot or treat eating disorders, and some might even lack knowledge of this group of mental illnesses altogether.

In another alarming development, young girls all over the world are resorting to diet pills and other types of drugs to boost their weight loss. Some of the most dangerous ones contain various combinations of fenfluramine and phentermine, which can cause heart damage.

The Lure of Western Culture

Western 'culture' is not just a set of ideas but a whole constellation of ideas, concepts, images, practices, customs, material culture, technology, and other everyday factors that feed into these disorders, even when they are 'expressions of psychological conflict.' Certainly in terms of global diet and bodily culture, Western ideas are not the only factors affecting global change: technological, commercial, economic, agronomical, demographic, educational, and even mechanical (in terms of access to transport) changes are also influencing how bodies are changing internationally. We shouldn't be too surprised that [disordered], hypervigilant eating becomes more prevalent when food ways are in such a state of upheaval, body images are raining down on these populations, activity patterns are shifting, and so many of the new choices are unhealthy, fattening, and alien.

Greg Downey,
"Exporting American Mental Illness,"
Neuroanthropology *(blog),*
January 10, 2010. http://neuroanthropology.net.

Is the West to Blame?

In his book *Crazy Like Us: The Globalization of the American Psyche*, Ethan Watters suggests that eating disorders have gone global in tandem with the economy.

> There is now good evidence to suggest that in the process of teaching the rest of the world to think like us, we've been exporting our Western 'symptom repertoire' as well.[. . .] Indeed, a handful of mental health disorders—depression, post-traumatic stress disorder and anorexia among them—now appear to be spreading across cultures with the speed of contagious diseases.

In the last ten plus years, the mentality of the Chinese people has changed as drastically as their lifestyle. Those living in the fast-paced urban hubs, while maybe more comfortably than would have been possible a few decades ago, are now under a lot of pressure due to increasing competition for jobs and living space, and are finding themselves battling the same demons as people in the West have for decades. At the core of the problem seems to lay a human tendency to focus all attention on himself when he no longer needs to struggle for survival. And the easy way of life, obviously, is a consequence of modern advances, which also happen to mean an ease of access to food, best illustrated by the growing popularity of Western fast food across the globe. It seems that in this age of plenty, in the richer parts of the world, people sometimes develop a distorted view of themselves, according to which they are never successful or attractive enough to count among the prime specimens of their species.

One of the most pressing problems in China now is that eating disorders are spreading faster than the health care sector can keep up.

This is why in China, too, young and already-thin women hog down diet pills and sign up for weight loss programs even when they have no medical reasons for losing weight. As for why a thin or downright emaciated figure has come to represent the standard of beauty, we can only point at factors related to the development of the modern civilization, and which would take a whole book to detail. One of the most pressing problems in China now is that eating disorders are spreading faster than the health care sector can keep up. Fortunately, however, local support groups and websites offering counseling are already starting to be established.

Raising Awareness

In order to increase public awareness about eating disorders, the Chinese media should also step up its reporting on this disturbing phenomenon. At the moment, most reports about eating disorders seem to be very case specific, usually only highlighting the circumstances of incidents where a person has died from an eating disorder, and describing the reactions of the victim's surviving family members.

It now seems safe to say that modern China, a country renowned for its healthy traditional diet, has in a sense fallen into the same trap as the West did during its rise. There eating disorders have left thousands of people dead and millions more locked in an endless battle to retain control of their lives against a potentially debilitating mental illness. While the problem has not yet reached quite the same proportions in China, the potential for an explosion of eating disorders like never before seen in the history of mankind is already there.

Viewpoint 5

Britain Needs to Address the Problem of Anorexia Porn Websites

Nicola Hobbs

Nicola Hobbs is a contributor to the Guardian. *In the following viewpoint, she reports that anorexic women in the United Kingdom are being exploited by pornography agencies specializing in anorexic images. Posing as anorexic women, porn agents cultivate friendships with anorexics and solicit explicit photos, which then end up on pro-anorexic pornography websites. Hobbs notes that these young women have no protection from online exploitation, and experts agree that measures should be taken. At the very least, Hobbs maintains, raising awareness of the problem would be a start.*

As you read, consider the following questions:

1. According to Optenet, by how much did the number of pro-ana websites increase between 2006 and 2008 globally?
2. What eating disorder has the highest mortality rate of all psychiatric illnesses?

Nicola Hobbs, "Anorexic Women Targeted by 'Super-Skinny' Porn Websites," *The Guardian*, April 5, 2011. www.guardiannews.com.

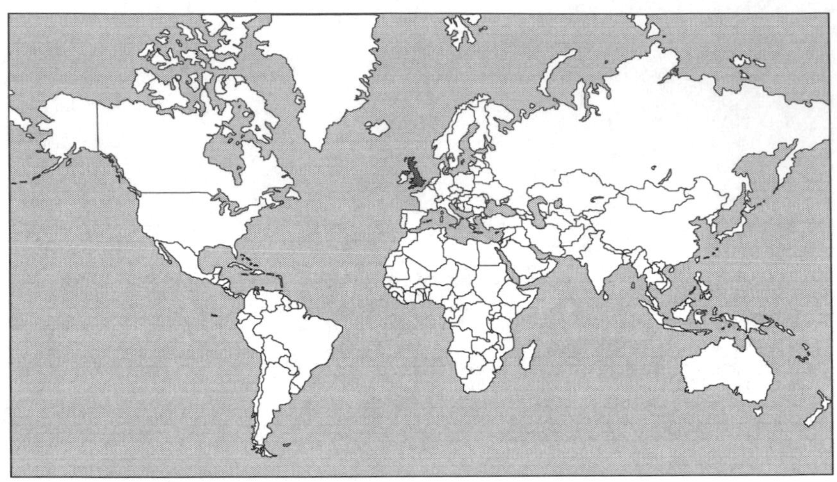

3. What does e-crime consultant Jennifer Perry recommend that the United Kingdom do to protect anorexic women?

"As you know, beauty has one name: being thin. Our models are underweight, skinny, thin, bony—just like you. We want you. Regardless of the costs, we want you to join our agency. Let's face facts, on anorexic porn websites, men are masturbating watching your pictures. You are a superstar of starvation and if you were selling and marketing your frame you would be more wealthy than most of us because men would pay any price for watching those pictures."

This was the e-mail Sasha McDonald was sent last year [2010] from a pornography agency specialising in anorexic images. McDonald was 15 when she was first diagnosed with anorexia nervosa. "I was very lonely and felt worthless," she says. "I retreated into an online pro-anorexic [pro-ana] community and shared everything. I didn't realise the danger I was putting myself under." Despite receiving professional support, McDonald found herself becoming more entrenched in the online anorexic world. She wrote a blog of her battle with anorexia, recording the small amounts she ate and publishing photographs of herself in her underwear as evidence of her emaciated body.

"I was dangerously underweight and so ill that I felt proud of the comments from other website users saying how beautiful and skinny my body was. I relied on the judgments of the friends I had made on pro-anorexia websites because I assumed they were people like me—scared, depressed, exhausted and battling an illness that torments you continuously," says McDonald.

Exploitation of Anorexic Girls

But McDonald was horrified when a fellow member of one pro-anorexia website e-mailed her requesting that she join a pornography agency. "My anorexic friend was actually a 46-year-old male with a fetish for skinny women," she says. "He had pretended to be a young girl and persuaded me to share sexually explicit pictures and tried to convince me to join his modelling agency for the super-skinny."

McDonald also found that emaciated photographs she had published of herself on her blog had been posted on anorexia porn forums for users with fetishes about super-skinny women to admire. "Beautiful girl—much prettier than all those meat mountains. Bones and ribs must be very visible. If their BMI [body mass index] is above 15, they are not attractive," says one forum user commenting on a skeletal photograph of McDonald.

Anorexia Porn

McDonald, now 19 and training to be a doctor, had recovered sufficiently to avoid being drawn into the world of anorexia porn, but others with eating disorders have not been so fortunate. Anorexia porn is growing in popularity and the prevalence of pro-anorexia websites is making those with eating disorders easy targets for grooming. Vulnerable users of pro-anorexia websites are increasingly being courted for their emaciated frames by pornography agencies specialising in images of extremely thin women. Optenet, an international IT [information technology] security company, reported that between 2006 and 2008 the number of pro-ana websites globally increased 470% to more than 1,500 and social networking and blogging has seen a surge in online pro-anorexia content.

One anorexia pornography agency admits to paying owners of pro-anorexia websites for each person who joins it after being contacted via the sites. "I pay the owner of this pro-ana community a donation for every model I found here," confesses a "skinny scout" in the e-mail to McDonald.

The Role of Porn Agency Websites

The porn agencies' websites have two roles. They sign up new clients and advertise images, films and escort-type services, such as body worshipping, fantasy role-play and private photography sessions, for those "hooked on skinnies". Some of this porn is free to access while other "professional" agencies charge a monthly membership fee for regularly updated sexually explicit images and videos of emaciated women. Agencies also host anorexia porn on YouTube and advertise on anorexia pornography forums.

These forums often offer advice on how to groom users of pro-anorexia websites into taking and sharing explicit photographs of themselves.

Anorexia nervosa has the highest mortality rate of all psychiatric illnesses, but in the UK [United Kingdom], those with the mental illness have no protection from online exploitation. The legality of anorexia porn means that indecent images of vulnerable adults can be freely published.

"It is government policy that controls a balance between freedom of expression and protection of the public on published material which should be proportionate to the potential harm that might be caused," says Justin Millar, a member of the Home Office's computer crime team. "The general test of obscenity is flexible, reflecting society's attitude towards pornographic material. But even if material is not illegal, it is open to anyone concerned about the content of pornography websites to ask the relevant Internet service provider to remove them."

The legality of anorexia porn means that indecent images of vulnerable adults can be freely published.

Lucky Escape

Samira Jay feels she had a lucky escape. Although she believes that pro-anorexia websites helped her to realise that she had a problem, Jay admits that she would never have published explicit photographs of herself if she had known that they were being used for sexual gratification. Now 19, and studying in Newcastle, she developed anorexia at 11. "It sickens me to the stomach knowing that my photographs could have been used for porn," she says.

"At the time, I was lonely and the pro-anorexia community gave me a purpose in life. Most users posted photographs of their naked bodies because when you have anorexia, the eating disorder is the only thing you feel you are good at, so it gives you a sense of achievement."

Experts agree that much more could be done. "Criminals and predators target vulnerable people online; they simply have no conscience about what they do. Vulnerable people are often not able to make good decisions for themselves and they need others to help protect them," says Jennifer Perry, an e-crime consultant.

"If the UK set the precedent of removing a set of offensive material it would encourage different countries to also take action. Currently, the most effective way to address this problem is education and discussing how people are being approached and exploited."

Many feel that much of the onus should fall on Internet service providers. "Responsible Internet service providers would remove the most hard-core and toxic material," says Susan Ringwood, chief executive of Beat, a UK eating disorder charity. "Pro-ana sites don't hold out any hope at all, they can trap people in a negative cycle of despair."

Jay acknowledges that she is not fully recovered, but she now speaks out about her historic use of pro-anorexia websites to make vulnerable people aware of the dangers of using them. "I knew my photographs might be used as 'thinspiration' by other eating disorder sufferers but the thought that they were being used for sexual enjoyment never even crossed my mind," she says.

Periodical and Internet Sources Bibliography

The following articles have been selected to supplement the diverse views presented in this chapter.

Clair Bates	"Teenage Girls Who Use Facebook 'Are More Likely to Become Anorexic,'" *Daily Mail* (UK), February 8, 2011.
BBC News	"Media Is Fuelling Eating Disorders, Say Psychiatrists," February 22, 2010. http://news.bbc.co.uk.
Jessica Bennett	"Does the Media Hate Women?," The Daily Beast, October 20, 2011. www.thedailybeast.com.
Harriet Brown	"The Media, Eating Disorders, and You," *Psychology Today*, November 19, 2010.
Lauren Cox	"Pro-Anorexia Websites Send Convoluted and Deadly Messages, Study Finds," ABC News, June 17, 2010. http://abcnews.go.com.
Hadley Freeman	"What Is the Link Between the Media and Eating Disorders?," *Guardian* (UK), August 2, 2011.
Leah Kraus	"Social Media Doesn't Help When It Comes to Eating Disorders," NCC News Online, February 15, 2011. https://nccnews.expressions.syr.edu.
Melissa Linton	"Teens & Eating Disorders: Is Social Media to Blame," Examiner.com, June 26, 2011. http://cdn2-b.examiner.com.
Alice Park	"How Social Networks Spread Eating Disorders," *Heartland* (blog), January 7, 2011. http://healthland.time.com.

Chapter 4

Strategies to Curb Eating Disorders

VIEWPOINT 1

Scotland Is Making Strides in Raising Awareness of Eating Disorders

Katie Mackintosh

Katie Mackintosh is a reporter for Holyrood. *In the following viewpoint, she contends that although experts believe Scotland has made great progress in the treatment of eating disorders, services are spotty across the country. There is a need to raise awareness of eating disorders among educators and students, Mackintosh asserts, to prevent misinformation and misunderstandings that hinder diagnoses and treatment. Furthermore, experts argue there must be treatment options available that cater to the needs of the Scottish people and a systematic evaluation process that identifies treatments that are particularly effective.*

As you read, consider the following questions:

1. According to Emma Healey, during what ages are young people most vulnerable to developing an eating disorder?
2. What group does the author say was instrumental in developing the National Health Service guidelines for the management and treatment of eating disorders in Scotland in 2006?

Katie Mackintosh, "The Push to Raise Awareness of Eating Disorders in Scotland," *Holyrood*, February 15, 2011. www.holyrood.com.

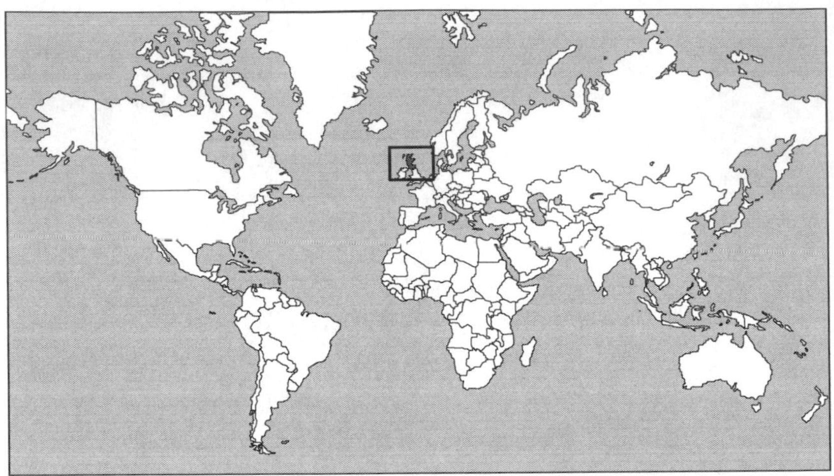

3. Why does the author say it has been hard to identify what is working in eating disorder treatment?

"When I was 14 I had an onset of depression. Six months or so later, I started to eat very little. It was a sudden idea on my part. Food had always been a problem in my mind but I became very sure I had to be thin and as quick as possible," explains one former anorexia sufferer.

She dropped weight quickly but her school, which at the time had the highest incidence of eating disorders in Scotland, was paying close attention so her dramatic weight loss did not go unnoticed. After battling the disorder for six years, during which period she spent time as a day [patient] and outpatient at an adolescent mental health clinic, "had a few scrapes with being sectioned", and was later referred to an adult clinic for CBT [cognitive behavioral therapy], she says she then chose to get well.

Getting Treatment

"I had a moment where I realised that basically nothing could feel worse than how I was feeling physically and emotionally. I was even willing to think that being overweight would be better than how incredibly unwell I felt. So I slowly started to eat and properly committed unlike my other 'recoveries' as a teenager." Individual stories like these show that eating disorders can be beaten, argues Beat, a UK [United Kingdom] charity for people with eating disorders and their families. However, a number of obstacles lie in the way and progress continues to be hampered by "patchy" service provision.

"Specialist services are poor across the UK and they are poor across Scotland too. There are a number of highly committed specialists working in the field. There are centres of excellence in Scotland. But people will still be receiving a very patchy service," explains Emma Healey, director of operations, Beat.

The Need for Better Understanding of Eating Disorders

Furthermore, she says a high level of misunderstanding and misinformation about eating disorders persists.

"Still some people, even health care professionals, don't understand that eating disorders are a mental health illness, which is terrifying. Still some people think that eating disorders are some sort of lifestyle choice, that it is something that you make happen, whether it is through dieting or whatever." Voluntary organisations are beginning to campaign for change but there is still more work to be done, she admits.

From 21 February [2011] Beat will be running a campaign for Eating Disorders Awareness Week, which this year will focus on how the media portrays people with such disorders. "One of the things that young people tell us is that they do not find the use of those graphic images of people when they are exceptionally thin and frail, they don't find them helpful, and I suppose what we are saying is that [it] is, perhaps, just another way of reinforcing the stigmas that people with eating disorders, particularly those with anorexia, face," says Healey.

Someone with an eating disorder can be desperately ill with compromised potassium and electrolyte levels and you may not even notice, she says.

"So it is an unhealthy message anyway and for a significant number of young people, it is highly triggering. And I suppose there is a concern that we are buying in to the fetish—the fetishisation of that very thin body and that is no better than some of the pro-ana [pro-anorexia] sites that you see." Such images also focus on the physical rather than psychological factors around eating disorders.

"What young people often say is, 'It was never about how thin I got. This isn't a real representation of my eating disorder. My eating disorder is what is going on in my head. It is about how I'm feeling.'" While Healey says there has been "brilliant" work around tackling stigma and furthering understanding of mental health in Scotland, she says she would like to see more of a concerted drive around child and adolescent mental health.

Starting Education Early

A good start would be ensuring that information about eating disorders is accessible in schools, she says.

"Too often in schools eating disorders get hidden," she says. "Young people don't feel that they can talk to the adults around them.

They are concerned that their teacher will tell their parents.

"But at the same time, there needs to be more information accessible at a school level because young people between the ages of 12–25 are the most vulnerable to developing an eating disorder." Similarly, she says that "tactless and insensitive" attitudes around weighing children in schools can give young people negative information about their body shape, which can cause issues for young people moving forward.

Eating Disorders in Scotland

- Anyone can develop an eating disorder, although most likely it will occur in young women aged 15 to 25
- Over 1.1 million people in the UK [United Kingdom] are directly affected by an eating disorder
- Recent research of young people in Scottish secondary schools showed that 68% recognise anorexia as a mental health problem. Only 9% considered someone with an eating disorder to be attention seeking
- Girls and women are 10 times more likely than boys and men to suffer from anorexia or bulimia
- Eating disorders affect 1 15-year-old girl in every 150 and 1 15-year-old boy in every 1000

"Eating Disorders," See Me, 2011. www.seemescotland.org.uk.

A Wide Range of Sufferers

However, it is important to remember that eating disorders affect people at opposite ends of the spectrum.

"What we know from our adult services is that a significant number of people who would be defined as obese either have a diagnosable eating disorder or certainly have an emotionally unhealthy attitude to food. So the health service needs to ask itself some complicated questions about if you are putting people through very invasive procedures like bariatric surgery, are you providing all the help that they need to actually manage that and sustain it. Because actually giving someone a gastric band is not going to make them eat healthily, and if you are not dealing with the issues around depression, [and] isolation, it can be very difficult." While Beat predominantly works in England and Wales it is hoping to start carrying out more specific work in Scotland this year. Together with NHS [National Health Service] Tayside and the University of Dundee, last month [January 2011] it was involved in relaunching the Eating Disorders Network in Dundee, which aims to promote self-help and peer support for adults who are experiencing any kind of eating disorder, locally, and hopes a similar initiative in St Andrews will begin shortly.

It is important to remember that eating disorders affect people at opposite ends of the spectrum.

They are also planning to pilot a virtual self-help group in the Scottish Borders, to see how technology could be used to widen access to support. Healey says she also hopes Beat can continue its strong links with the Scottish Eating Disorder Interest Group (SEDIG) to make sure support is on the ground and push for change.

A Scottish Solution

Dr Jane Morris, chair, SEDIG, reciprocates and says Beat will be very welcome in Scotland.

"We are very keen to find a specifically Scottish solution to our eating disorders difficulties," Morris says.

"Down in England they have a very different mental health act. A different children's act so that the management of young people and the average age of onset is only 15. So it is very important that our education system, our legal system, as well as our cultural system, which is very much more NHS than private hospitals, is taken into account."

There have been some "absolutely enormous" improvements in tackling eating disorders in Scotland in recent years, she argues. Some of the SEDIG group—which Morris describes as a "unique" collaboration between patients and their lay and professional carers, including professionals from the public and private sector—were involved in developing the NHS QIS [Quality Improvement Scotland] guidelines for the management and treatment of eating disorders in Scotland in 2006, which, she says, led to a number of positive developments in services in Scotland; while the establishment of Eating Disorders Education and Training Scotland (EEATS) to promote improved training for those providing care and treatment for eating disorders has also stimulated demand among professionals.

"We've now got two private hospitals offering inpatient treatment for eating disorders and I think the fact that there has been private provision, which the NHS has had to buy into, has also helped stimulate the NHS to open its own services. We already have the first inpatient eating disorders NHS unit in Aberdeen and there is going to be one in Livingston, probably open later this year." However, while those close to eating disorders can note these changes, a paucity of Scottish evidence makes it hard to say definitively what is working and why.

Better Research Is Needed

"Scottish eating disorders research is very far behind the wonderful academic record we have in things like psychosis or even depression or post-traumatic stress," says Morris.

"There are evidence-based treatments but they don't actually lead to recovery in any more than half of all the patients. So we do still need to keep exploring." Similarly, statistics showing the number of people seeking medical consultations for eating disorders only give a glimpse of the true extent to which eating disorders are affecting people in Scotland. However, Morris maintains that progress is evident in the increasing openness and awareness.

"A huge amount of progress has been made in terms of awareness and as a result, demand is now coming out of the closets, as it were. People and their families are seeking help in a way that they used not to. Eating disorders people are often for a long time very ambivalent about the prospect of help because they realise that it will involve sacrificing their weight-losing behaviours, and that is terrifying. So compared with other patients who are actively seeking help, it tends to be carers and people who are concerned who try to push people towards getting treatment, but we are now seeing a lot more openness."

VIEWPOINT 2

An Argentinean Social Movement Combats the Nation's Thin-Obsessed Culture

Joe Goldman

Joe Goldman is a reporter for ABC News. In the following viewpoint, he investigates the Feo, or ugly, campaign in Argentina, a country with a well-known beauty- and weight-obsessed culture. Feo promotes body acceptance, healthier body images in the marketplace and fashion industry, and less of an emphasis on looks. Goldman argues that many hope the Feo campaign and other measures can combat the high rate of anorexia and bulimia in Argentina and lessen the stigma of not being beautiful or thin.

As you read, consider the following questions:

1. According to Gonzalo Otalora, how many hits has the Feo website received from October–November 2007?
2. What size clothing do most clothing stories in Buenos Aires stock, according to the author?
3. What percentage of a company's employees does Otalora recommend be ugly?

Joe Goldman, "An Ugly Argentine Fights Back," ABCNews.com, November 13, 2007. abcnews.go.com.

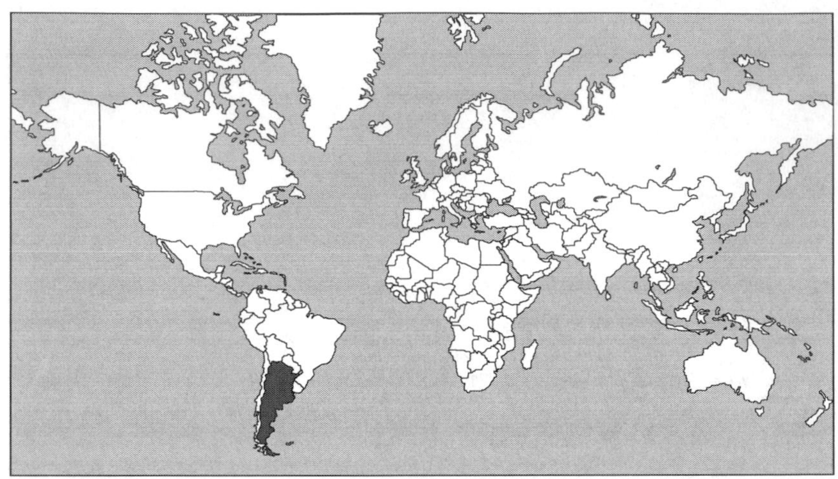

A beauty tax that grants subsidies to ugly people. Weekly marches through the downtown streets demanding equal treatment for those handicapped by not being good-looking.

All spurned by a runaway best-selling book called *Ugly* [*¡Feo!*] that is filling up bookstore windows all over town.

There are bumper stickers too, and posters are filling the streets and subway cars that replicate the famed Rolling Stones' Andy Warhol–designed mouth with the tongue sticking out, but with one change. These teeth have braces!

All this is occurring in, of all places, the fashion-conscious, aesthetics-obsessed, plastic surgery capital of the world—Buenos Aires.

The Feo Movement

Gonzalo Otalora is the author of the book and leader of the movement called Feo, which means ugly in Spanish.

ABC News met up recently with Otalora as he and some followers marched down Florida Street, the busy central Buenos Aires walkway, gathering signatures for their petition to tax the gorgeous.

Otalora presented his case to inquisitive passersby while holding a megaphone aloft and shouting slogans like: "Don't think of your body as commercial packaging!" and "Ideal beauty is a fraud!"

The Response to Feo

"Since we published the book, the repercussions have been tremendous," Otalora told ABC News.

"Just on the Web site [www.feosexual.com] we have had over 20,000 hits in just a few weeks," said the 30-something TV and radio producer who, while not exactly a poster boy, is not the image one perceives as the leader of the ugly movement.

He's a bit pudgy with a somewhat receding hairline, but his reddish, sparse beard and angular features make one think of a young, miniature Richard Dreyfuss.

"Hundreds of the responses on the Web site are long personal accounts from people who have suffered tremendously with their physical features since childhood," said Otalora who admits that writing the book was therapy for him.

"I was a skinny kid with thick, horn-rimmed glasses, acne and just plain ugly," said Otalora showing his picture in the book's inner jacket. Indeed his childhood photo, which blesses, well, confronts the reader who opens the book, shows a prototypical class nerd from sixth grade.

A Shallow, Beauty-Obsessed Culture

Argentina is said to have one of the highest rates of plastic surgery per capita in the world. A decade ago ABC's *20/20* interviewed Jose Juri, one of the leading Argentine plastic surgeons, for a special segment on the subject. Juri was taped while he performed a nose reconstruction procedure. In the middle of the operation, he turned to the camera, scalpel in hand, and blurted out, "when it comes to the nose, I'm Michelangelo!"

In a society where so much weight is placed on physical beauty, doctors like Juri have indeed been put on a pedestal. And more so these days with Argentina being one of the cheapest countries in the world, plastic surgeons' offices are flooded with foreigners looking for good, but cheap procedures.

Anorexia and bulimia are also huge problems in a society where image is so important. Even mannequins in dress shop windows appear to have eating disorders.

[The ugly] campaign appears to have struck a raw nerve in a nation that has been undergoing huge changes over the last decades. However, in the end, it may be a hard sell.

A Law That Makes Sense

A few years ago the Buenos Aires city council passed a law requiring women's clothing retailers to offer a wide range of sizes instead of the skimpy size 2s prevalent in all establishments.

Even though the law is on the books and even though it makes complete economic sense to sell all sizes, many stores have not complied with the law and there is virtually no enforcement.

"When it comes to weight and body types we should do a census to find out who we really are. We certainly are not what the clothing stores portray," said Otalora. "And combine that with everything else, the diets, the laser treatments, the makeup, the hair transplants, hair dyes, colored contact lenses and all kinds of beauty potions. It's crazy!"

New Proposals

Undeterred, Otalora is proposing a slew of new laws that would deal with the problem and include the following ideas:

- Companies must ensure that at least 30 percent of their employees are ugly (including public relations, receptionists and executives)
- Thirty percent of the casts of the soap operas should be ugly and at least one of the lead characters should specifically not be attractive
- In fashion shows, all sizes and physical qualities should be represented. Mannequins should represent all sizes and physical qualities
- Advertising should represent all sizes and different physical characteristics
- Sex magazines should be obliged to have ugly and fat people as models
- Beautiful and ugly persons should receive equal pay
- Advertising should abstain from using touch-ups, trick lighting, makeup or whatever other effect that modifies the true body or face of the model

Otalora's campaign appears to have struck a raw nerve in a nation that has been undergoing huge changes over the last decades. However, in the end, it may be a hard sell.

One woman who refused to sign the petition on Florida Street commented that she didn't have time. With a smirk she explained, "I'm on my way to the beauty parlor."

VIEWPOINT 3

Israel Is Considering a Bill to Ban Underweight Fashion Models

Liat Collins

Liat Collins is the editor of the International Jerusalem Post. *In the following viewpoint, she reports on a new bill being considered by the Israeli government that would prohibit fashion agencies from employing underweight fashion models. In addition, Collins explains, it would force photos of fashion models that have been altered to make the women seem skinnier than they really are to carry a notice revealing that. Collins contends that healthy fashion models and more realistic body images in the media are a step toward confronting the serious problem of eating disorders in Israel.*

As you read, consider the following questions:

1. According to Adi Barkan, how many female models are working in Israel?
2. What percentage of Israeli fashion models suffer from undernourishment, according to Barkan?
3. How much smaller does Barkan say that Israeli fashion models are than they were ten–twelve years ago?

Liat Collins, "Real Israel: Slim Pickings," *Jerusalem Post*, June 25, 2010. www.jpost.com.

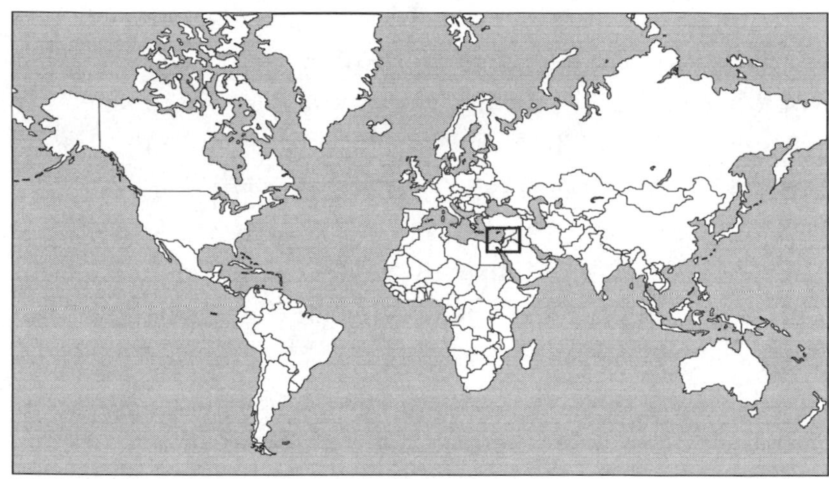

Will the country's fashion models become lifesaving role models? This was the heavy topic being discussed in the cabinet and Knesset [legislature] last week [June 2010] around the preliminary reading of a bill aimed at reducing the number of superthin models suffering from larger-than-life eating disorders.

The bill, which could make "heroin chic" a bad trip down memory lane, was initiated by Kadima [a political party] MK [member of Knesset] Rachel Adatto, a physician, and Likud MK Danny Danon, who chairs the Knesset Committee on the Rights of the Child. But the man putting all his weight behind it is Adi Barkan, who runs one of the country's most successful modeling agencies. After taking a break from the business for a few years, Barkan made a comeback with his Simply U agency which makes a point of employing only models who pass a weight test.

A Change of Heart

Barkan admits he is making up for past sins by pushing for the legislation and social change that shows that beauty is more than skin deep.

Hungry for success, most models would eat their hearts out for a good contract. But they wouldn't eat real food. That would change if Barkan has his way. His commitment only deepened when, in 2007, 33-year-old Hila Elmalich died in his arms as he rushed the anorexic model to the hospital.

There are some 200–300 female models working in the country, he says. "More than 70 percent of them suffer from undernourishment. They would rather their periods stop than add a kilogram. We're talking about a life-and-death matter."

Hungry for success, most models would eat their hearts out for a good contract. But they wouldn't eat real food.

Barkan talks with passion. He's been promoting his "Be Beautiful and Stay Alive" campaign for close to a decade. Five-and-a-half years ago, a similar bill backed by MK Inbal Gavrieli was discussed, but the Knesset was dispersed before it came up for a vote in the plenum. "I think this is the last chance we have of saving these lives," says Barkan of the latest bill which breezed through preliminary reading.

"This is not New York," says Barkan. "The market is small." There are basically only five or six influential modeling agencies in the country.

"This is the No 1. prevention plan. It won't cost much money and it will be easy to enforce. The Ministry of Industry, Trade and Labor has already agreed to help with the enforcement."

Examining the Bill

The bill is a thing of beauty, taking a two-pronged approach. First, agencies will not be allowed to employ models who do not provide a doctor's certificate attesting they are not underweight, defined by a body mass index of less than 18.5. And photos which have been altered by Photoshop to make the

How Adi Barkan Became an Activist

Adi Barkan, an Israeli photographer and model agent, became acutely aware of the pervasiveness of anorexia when he interviewed 12,000 females aged 13 to 24 in a televised search for Israel's next supermodel. He estimated that between 35 and 40% of these aspiring models were anorexic. This realisation, combined with repeated encounters with the illness, persuaded him to launch a crusade to combat it within his industry.

Conal Urquhart,
"Shaping a Nation,"
Guardian, *July 14, 2005.*

models look thinner will have to carry a notice to that effect, somewhat like the "Smoking can endanger your health" warnings on cigarette packets.

A Serious Problem

While the success of Israeli models abroad has grown over the years, the size of the models has shrunk, Barkan notes. "Today's models are about two sizes smaller than those who worked a decade or 12 years ago. Those two sizes are the critical difference between a healthy, slim and sexy model and one suffering from the plague of deadly eating disorders," Barkan states.

When I mention a book I have just reviewed on Marilyn Monroe, Barkan laughs dryly and quips: "She wouldn't even get a job selling cosmetics in a supermarket today."

Barkan hopes that the message of healthy models conveyed in the law will be carried around the world, and there has been international interest in the initiative.

Much of the problem lies with those dying to get into the business. "Would-be models turn up for an audition and are told to lose five kilos," says Barkan. "But, of course, it never stops there. They keep on dieting and keep on losing weight. A girl who gets into such a cycle is emotionally dead from Day 1."

Including the Whole Industry

Barkan is also trying to make photographers see the bigger picture. "The fashion scene is dominated by gay photographers and their tastes are not for . . . bums," Barkan says.

Altogether, admitting that change has to come at a societal level rather than simply through legislation, Barkan has been actively recruiting major advertisers such as the Strauss food giant and the Castro fashion chain to back the cause by using "healthy" models. "Once I've explained the situation to the marketing personnel or CEOs [chief executive officers], most get the point," says Barkan.

While the public can probably relate more to the normal-size model—how many of us can say we've shrunk two sizes in the last decade, after all—at the moment you have a fat chance of finding them.

"When the day comes that a talent scout tells a girl, 'You're too skinny,' we'll know we have succeeded in getting our message across," Barkan states.

Barkan hopes to change the lives and perceptions of more than just the wannabe [Israeli model] Bar Refaelis. He wants young girls (and boys) and perhaps also their parents to see healthy role models also in key positions in the entertainment industry and on TV where the superthin still rule, creating an unhealthy example.

"It's a small country. Change is possible," says Barkan.

But it's clear the battle won't be over until the fat lady sings.

VIEWPOINT 4

France Considers Legislation to Outlaw the Promotion of Excessive Thinness

Lisa Abend and Susan Sachs

Lisa Abend and Susan Sachs are correspondents for the Christian Science Monitor. *In the following viewpoint, they examine a French bill that makes it a crime for publications, modeling agencies, or fashion designers to promote extreme thinness or extreme dieting. The bill also prohibits websites that encourage eating disorders. Abend and Sachs view this as part of the European trend to creatively address the epidemic of eating disorders among young women. Although many experts applaud the measures, others think that it will have limited effectiveness, according to the authors.*

As you read, consider the following questions:

1. According to the French bill, how much can a publication, modeling agency, or fashion designer be fined for "inciting" anorexia?
2. How many young women in Spain do the authors say are affected by eating disorders?
3. According to Abend and Sachs, what percentage of Spanish apparel manufacturers agreed to standardize their female clothing sizes?

Lisa Abend and Susan Sachs, "France Turns to Fines, Jail to Combat Ultrathin Ideals," *Christian Science Monitor*, April 17, 2008.

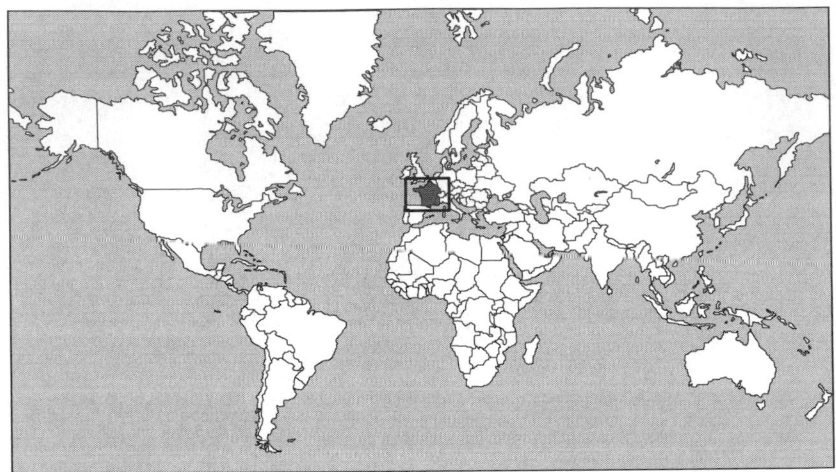

A young woman with flagging self-worth, she already had enough to grapple with in Paris, where fashion dictates ultrathin ideals.

"I've lost 12 kilos [26 pounds], but I feel heavy," wrote a blogger identifying herself only as Leila this month [April 2008] in an online journal devoted to her eating disorder. "Heavy, and at the same time, empty."

France Takes Action

But the fact that Leila's blog advocates anorexia has made her something of an outlaw overnight. On Tuesday [April 15, 2008], France's lower house of parliament passed a bill that makes it a crime to promote "excessive thinness" or extreme dieting.

Coming on the heels of related initiatives in Spain and Italy, the ban is the latest and most far-reaching attempt to stem a disorder—and an image of womanhood—with which hundreds of thousands of Europeans wrestle. But how effective will the measures—and some are quite creative—be?

France's bill, which must now be approved by the Senate, won unanimous support from [President] Nicolas Sarkozy's ruling UMP [Union for a Popular Movement] party, empowers judges to punish with prison terms and fines of up to €45,000 [euros] ($72,000) any publication, modeling agency, or fashion designer who "incites" anorexia. It also allows for the prosecution of websites whose pages and blogs, like Leila's, promote eating disorders.

The ban is the latest and most far-reaching attempt to stem a disorder—and an image of womanhood—with which hundreds of thousands of Europeans wrestle.

On these sites, young women chart behavior associated with anorexia, in which individuals driven by a deep-seated fear of weight gain deprive themselves of food, and bulimia, characterized by binge eating and purging. The sites—part of a growing genre of sites that glorify destructive eating patterns—offer encouragement, contests, and tricks for those attempting to starve themselves.

"The sociocultural and media environment seems to favor the emergence of troubled nutritional behavior, and that is why I think it necessary to act," said Valérie Boyer, the lawmaker who proposed the bill, in an interview with the Associated Press.

Several prominent French families, including former president Jacques Chirac's, have raised awareness of the issue by going public about their anorexic daughters' struggles.

A Global Problem

But the problem is hardly limited to France. "The rates of anorexia and bulimia are fairly constant across Europe and the United States," says Eric van Furth, clinical director of the Center for Eating Disorders Ursula in the Netherlands and former president of the Academy for Eating Disorders. "Genetics plays a significant role, but the environment—and that includes culture—helps determine whether those genes are expressed."

The Fate of the French Bill

In 2008 the French Parliament took action as the number of pro–eating disorder websites rose. Valérie Boyer, *a député* from the Bouches-du-Rhóne region of France, presented a bill in the French National Assembly calling for a prohibition on material that "provokes a person to seek excessive thinness by encouraging prolonged restriction of nourishment." The proposed legislation imposed a fine of €30,000 [euros] ($44,784) and two years imprisonment. This penalty rose to €45,000, or $67,176, and three years if there was a resulting death. The bill passed through the National Assembly but was stalled in the Senate where in June 2008, it was recommended that the bill was defeated and replaced with early eating disorder screening programs run by schools and physicians.

Emma Morris,
"Self-Harm in the Digital Age,"
FOSI Report, *2010.*

In Spain, where some experts say that eating disorders affect 1 in 200 young women, the country's major fashion show provoked controversy two years ago when it tried to address the issue. Banning from the catwalk models with an unhealthily low body mass index (or BMI—a weight to height ratio) of below 18, the vice councilwoman for the economy in Madrid's regional government, Concha Guerra, said, "Our intention is to promote good body image by using models whose bodies match reality and reflect healthy eating habits."

Milan followed suit, requiring a BMI of at least 18.5 for all models in its prominent fashion shows. And although organizers of London Fashion Week refused to enact a similar restriction, they did require all models to present a certificate from an eating disorder specialist that attested to their good health.

Other Efforts

There have been other creative efforts in Europe to reduce the media presence of the ultrathin and bring standards of female beauty in closer alignment with real, healthy women.

In the Netherlands, Unilever agreed to restrict models in its advertising campaigns to women with BMIs between 18 and 25. Last month [March 2008], Italy's health and sports ministries launched a campaign that, in addition to providing eating disorder education in the schools, provides media guidelines intended to discourage ultrathin beauty ideals. That campaign came just months after one of the country's clothing labels began its own anti-anorexia campaign with billboards depicting the nude, emaciated body of anorexic French model Isabelle Caro.

In Spain, the national government is taking a more positive approach. It recently persuaded 90 percent of the country's apparel manufacturers to agree to standardize their female clothing sizes. The new sizes will be based on a study, conducted under the auspices of the ministry of health, that measured the shape and size of 8,000 Spanish girls and women between the ages of 10 and 70. By making clothing sizes for real women's bodies, says Angeles Heras, general director of the ministry's consumer office, "the measure promotes a healthy model of beauty." So, too, she says, does another provision of the agreement, which prevents shops from using display mannequins smaller than a size 38 (US size 6).

Philippe Jeammet, a Paris psychiatrist and author of several books on eating disorders, supports the new French legislation and other measures that question fashion and the media's celebration of ultrathinness. "I think it's time for our society, which has benefited for so long from so much freedom, to start to think about limits. With respect to our children, we can't accept any glorification of destructive behavior."

Debate on the Law's Efficacy

But other experts question whether the French law by itself will have a significant impact. Janet Treasure, director of the Eating Disorders Unit at King's College London's Institute of Psychiatry, notes that although the law "may be helpful," there are many reasons why an individual may struggle with anorexia and bulimia—media images are just part of it.

Dr. van Furth, who classifies the disorders as mental illnesses, sees the main value of the French law as alerting the public to the issue. "[It's] a clear sign to society that we need to do things differently when we present these ideals to women," he says. But he nevertheless agrees that media and the fashion industry are only part of the problem and admits that he has "great doubts that legislation like this can be enforced."

He also worries that the provision that criminalizes websites advocating eating disorders and abetting such behavior is misplaced. "I don't think it's smart to punish the sufferers," he says. "The websites are part of their illness."

Viewpoint 5

The Japanese Government Needs to Launch a Campaign to Fight Eating Disorders

Terrie Lloyd

Terrie Lloyd is a businessperson, commentator, and writer. In the following viewpoint, he points out that although the Japanese launched an antiobesity campaign in 2008, it has yet to significantly address the high rate of eating disorders in the nation. Another problem in Japan is the pervasive media images that reinforce distorted body images and promote extreme thinness. Lloyd underscores the fact that Japanese women are lighter today on average than they were after World War II when there were widespread food shortages.

As you read, consider the following questions:

1. According to the Japanese health ministry, what percentage of women aged twenty–forty years old are underweight?
2. How many young people does the author say died from anorexia in Japan in 2003?
3. According to a 2008 health ministry survey, what percentage of Japanese women consider themselves fat?

Terrie Lloyd, "The Flip Side of Metabolic Syndrome—Being Too Skinny," *Japan Inc.*, March 28, 2010. www.japaninc.com.

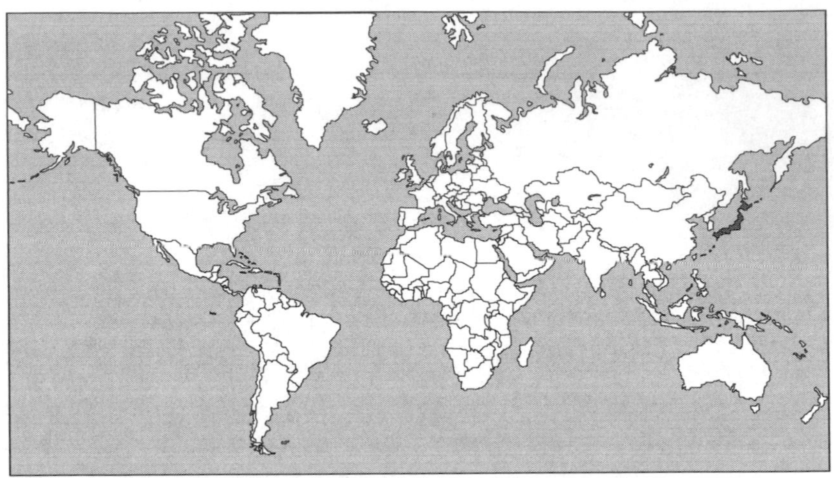

The week before last [in March 2010], Fast Retailing's Uniqlo brand said that it is experiencing a big boom in women's fashion leggings, and will be expanding its lineup from less than 10 styles last year to 107 styles this year. Uniqlo makes thin but collectively massive margins from knowing what consumers want, and this year they want the thin look—so you can be sure that leggings, most commonly worn with miniskirts, are going to be big this season.

OK, so big deal, the streets are going to feature some more eye candy, but how is this meaningful to the rest of us (i.e., women who don't wear leggings and almost all men)? Well, we started thinking about those leggings and why they are so popular. For sure the main attraction is that as a young or young-at-heart female you get to show off your legs without feeling embarrassed. This is certainly the marketing message, and anyone with a bit of fat on their thighs needn't buy them.

The Media and Eating Disorders

The thing is that we started noticing just how many girls wearing leggings seem to be thin as rakes—starved in fact. And this made us wonder whether the advertising being pumped out by the fashion and health industries isn't actually causing consumers to have an increased rate of eating disorders—which certainly are a problem outside Japan, amongst young women in particular.

Just look around you and you will realize that everywhere in Japan the message to consumers is "skinny is in". Skinny leggings, skinny fit jeans, even the government wants us to be skinny with its anti-Metabo (Metabolic Syndrome) campaign [a campaign to fight obesity] introduced in April 2008. Yes, being obese is not healthy, but are we going too far in the opposite direction?

According to the health ministry, the average weight of women in their 30s dropped 12% over the period 1986–2006, and now 20% of all women aged 20 through 40 are in fact underweight. It's hard to believe, but the ministry made the point that at present Japanese women are now lighter on average than they were after World War II when there was a shortage of food!

Just look around you and you will realize that everywhere in Japan the message to consumers is "skinny is in".

The two main eating disorders contributing to excessively low weight are anorexia nervosa and bulimia nervosa. With anorexia, sufferers are critical of their own body appearance and continually want to lose weight. Methods of doing this include obsessive avoidance of fattening foods, obsessive use of dieting aids, vomiting after a meal, excessive use of laxatives, etc. Wikipedia says that anorexics are the most likely out of people with psychological disturbances to commit suicide—and we don't doubt that this fact contributed to the 26 or so kids (mainly girls) who apparently died from the condition in Japan in 2003.

What Is the Metabo Law?

Those [Japanese men and women] exceeding government [waistline] limits—33.5 inches for men and 35.4 inches for women, which are identical to thresholds established in 2005 for Japan by the International Diabetes Federation as an easy guideline for identifying health risks—and having a weight-related ailment will be given dieting guidance if after three months they do not lose weight. If necessary, those people will be steered toward further reeducation after six more months.

Norimitsu Onishi,
"Japan, Seeking Trim Waists, Measures Millions,"
New York Times, *June 13, 2008.*

Raising Awareness

Actually 2003 was a year of awareness of anorexia in Japan. Keio University did their first survey on the disease and found that about 2% of all female high school seniors suffered from the condition, although only 0.6% had actually been diagnosed by doctors. Outside that 2%, apparently another 10% were considered close to developing the disorder. The survey was accompanied by a report noting that excessive dieting for teenagers is more harmful to their health than smoking and drinking, and that between 10%–20% of anorexics go on to early deaths because of various bodily dysfunctions caused by semipermanent starvation.

While one normally thinks of anorexia as a teenager disease, the problem appears to be spreading to women in their 40s and 50s as well. A 2008 health ministry survey found that 12.6% of thin women with a BMI [body mass index] under 18.5 (only 20% of Japanese women are considered obese) are still trying to lose weight and that a full 52.6 percent of all women consider themselves fat. Perhaps this has to do with the fact that more women are staying single later in life and therefore are still very susceptible to advertising messages.

The Diet Industry in Japan

Dieting is of course a big business worldwide, and nowhere more so than in Japan. Despite the recent economic downturn the demand for diet aids and food supplements has continued to grow. We don't have access to specific recent numbers for the diet industry itself, but back in 2001 a Ministry of Economy, Trade and Industry (METI) council reckoned that the functional health food market would be worth around JPY3.2trn [3.2 trillion Japanese yen] by this year and in 2005 the *Kenko Sangyo* newspaper estimated the market at that time to be worth 630bn [billion]. So it's probably a fair guess to say that functional foods, much of which is taken up by the diet industry, is probably worth at least JPY1trn to JPY1.5trn by now.

One sector of the dieting industry which certainly is doing well is that of health metering equipment. Panasonic has just introduced a calorie calculator called the Day Calorie, and while they were expecting a few hundred sales on introducing the new product on their website, in fact they had requests for over 2,200 units. Needless to say, Panasonic will be ramping up its manufacturing volumes. Pedometers from Omron and other makers' exercise devices are also selling well.

Weighing scales maker Tanita is already selling calorie counters and apparently has sold more than 70,000 units since April 2009. This April, the company plans to introduce a super-duper new device called the InnerScan 50, which will measure weight, body fat percentage, muscle mass, and the condition of your wallet . . . (ok, maybe not the last bit). But the InnerScan *will* come with a memory card that you can plug into your PC [personal computer]. Using the Tanita application software, you can then obsessively monitor your weight/fitness progress before and after using laxatives and dieting powders. We think it will be a big hit.

According to the Nikkei [a stock market index], currently Tanita, Panasonic, and other makers sell about 2.5m [million] home-use health monitoring devices a year.

Japan Needs to Do a Better Job

So while we applaud the government's focus on trimming waistlines so as to reduce (mainly men's) heart disease and other later-stage diseases, it is a fact that anorexia can cause equally severe health problems, such as various heart, blood sugar, bone, mental, and other malnutrition-related conditions that shorten life span and put a load on the nation's health system. Thus we find it strange that the health ministry doesn't run a similarly high-profile campaign to target women who are obsessed with keeping their weight abnormally low.

And until that happens, we presume that Uniqlo is going to be selling an awful lot of leggings.

Viewpoint 6

New Zealand Has Stepped Up Its Eating Disorders Treatment Programs

Jonathan Coleman

Jonathan Coleman is immigration minister in New Zealand. In the following viewpoint, he maintains that New Zealand has made a concerted effort to improve mental health services since 2007, when a government assessment revealed that a number of young women suffering from eating disorders had to travel to Australia for treatment because New Zealand did not provide adequate resources. Coleman outlines the improvements, which involve centers of specialization and then primary care in smaller provincial centers. These improvements will allow patients to receive specialized care and treatment close to home.

As you read, consider the following questions:

1. What percentage of New Zealanders does Coleman say suffer from eating disorders?
2. How much did the New Zealand government add to eating disorders services funding starting in 2009, according to the author?

Dr. Jonathan Coleman, "Speech to the Annual Conference of the Australia and New Zealand Academy for Eating Disorders," beehive.govt.nz, August 27, 2010.

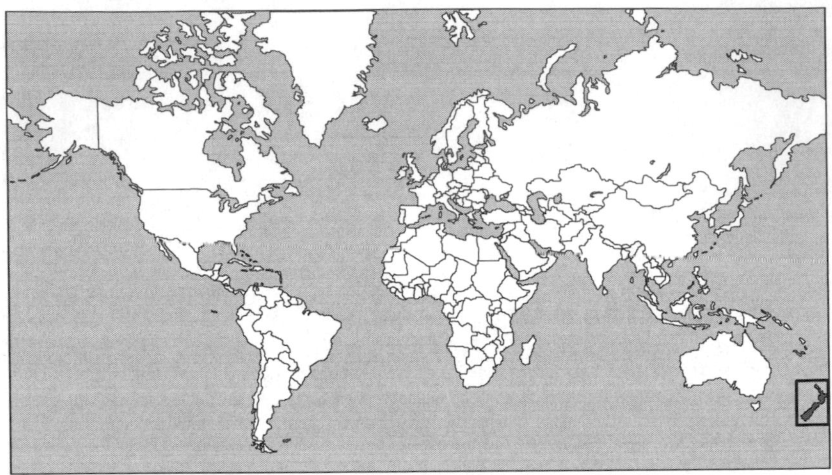

3. What three New Zealand cities does Coleman say will be the hubs of care provision when it comes to eating disorders?

It is an honour to be here at the 8th annual conference of the Australia and New Zealand Academy for Eating Disorders [ANZAED] and the first such conference to be held here in New Zealand. This move is timely, as much-needed progress has recently been made here to improve our eating disorders services in New Zealand.

I know you're interested to hear about those changes, particularly on those here in Auckland. First though I think it's important to remember what the environment for eating disorders in New Zealand has been like just to place into context the improvement made in a relatively short period.

Positive Changes

In 2007, the Mental Health Commission undertook a stock take of mental health services, including eating disorders services. The commission found that there were considerable problems with access to eating disorders services, evidenced by a lack of beds and long waiting lists. There were also next to no inpatient or residential care for people seriously ill with eating disorders in the Northern region.

As you all know, eating disorders are complex and encompass a range of conditions that have overlapping psychiatric and medical symptoms. The impact on the individual and their family is immense.

Mortality rates for eating disorders are high and around 1.7 percent of New Zealanders suffer from the illness. Having to seek treatment overseas would only serve to compound the situation, and it's estimated more than 20 people have been sent to Sydney for treatment since 2007 due to the lack of facilities in New Zealand.

An Encouraging Story

One of those people was an 18-year-old whose plight was reported in last Saturday's [in August 2010] *Weekend Herald*. Two years ago she was eating only half a grapefruit a day, had lost 10kg [kilograms] in two weeks and at the height of her illness she weighed only 33.7kg. She was referred to the local eating disorders service here in Auckland, but due to a three-month wait list and the seriousness of her condition, she was sent to Sydney for treatment where she and her mother spent four and a half months. Thankfully today she's making progress and her weight has almost doubled.

But while we appreciate the support of our Australian colleagues and the quality of the services provided, the situation was less than ideal for her and other young Kiwis [residents of New Zealand] and their families in the same situation. People need the support of loved ones close to home when they are going through a deeply difficult time.

This is why, last month, the government was pleased to announce further progress for providing a new regional eating disorders service in the top half of the North Island.

Auckland DHB [District Health Board] has contracted Challenge Trust to set up a residential treatment facility and day programme by the end of the year. The new services have been funded from an extra $26 million over four years that this government announced last year to improve eating disorders services nationwide.

Starship hospital established five new dedicated beds for children under 15 years with eating disorders last year as part of this extra funding. Challenge Trust's new facility will eventually include up to nine residential beds available for older adolescents and adults and will provide a homelike environment for patients, where they can spend time with their families.

The Auckland Regional Eating Disorders Service, working with these services, will act as a hub for service provision for patients from the Northern and Midland regions.

It is important to acknowledge that community-based services continue to provide the range of interventions that are essential to effective delivery of a continuum of care for eating disorders patients across the country.

Significant Improvements to Treatment Programs

While recent attention has been rightly directed toward developing inpatient and residential services here in Auckland, it is important to acknowledge that community-based services continue to provide the range of interventions that are essential to effective delivery of a continuum of care for eating disorders patients across the country.

Of the $26 million, around 80% has been allocated to improving services in the Northern and Midland regions as these were the regions with the least well-developed services. The remainder of the funding is being spread across the country and is providing other regions with extra and invaluable resources.

In the Central region new funding has been allocated to provide improved access to paediatric inpatient services for children and young people. The Central region has an existing six-bed residential service and day programme in Johnsonville, near Wellington.

In the Southern region new funding has been allocated to provide additional community eating disorders clinicians in Nelson Marlborough, Canterbury and Otago-Southland. Canterbury DHB has an existing seven-bed eating disorders inpatient unit serving the Southern region.

The additional funding will result in people having greater access to care and support across the country which is a significant improvement for the sector.

The Economic Backdrop

To provide some more context to the situation, we are just emerging from the worst global financial crisis in 70 years. New Zealand used to have large government surpluses but this week we borrowed $240 million and next week we will borrow another $240 million. We'll do the same every week after that for the next four years—just to keep public services like health ticking over.

Due to the economic constraints we continue to face, new spending across government has decreased or has been curtailed some in many areas.

In areas that impact heavily on people's lives however, the government has provided funding increases and health is the biggest single item of new operating spending in Budget 2010—up $512 million to $13.5 billion in 2010/11.

Health spending is now $1.4 billion a year more than when we came into government. An additional $2.1 billion is being invested in health priorities over the next four years.

Of that, District Health Boards will directly receive $1.4 billion extra over four years, and will also receive a large share of the extra funding going to targeted initiatives. Mental health funding increases by $40 million over the next four years and DHBs are expected to allocate $174 million from the new funding to mental health.

So while there will be a constant need to review where money is most effectively spent, and that will result in some reprioritisation across the sector, there is more money going into health than ever before. The problem here is that costs in health grow at a faster rate than our national income.

The ultimate aim must be to provide the best service and level of support for patients and their families in what is a very difficult time.

The Hub-and-Spoke Model

So given the difficult economic situation, we have to make targeted and intelligent use of the resources we have—which is what the hub-and-spoke model can offer.

This model also provides support closer to home for patients and their families.

In New Zealand, the hubs of care provision will be in Christchurch, Wellington and Auckland. The most specialised care will be provided in these centres.

Through regular contact, strong relationships and smart use of technology, specialists will be able to support primary and secondary eating disorders services throughout New Zealand.

In health, the aim is to facilitate clinical support by specialist clinicians in large regional centres (hubs) to clinicians in generic secondary services and, when appropriate, primary care in smaller provincial centres (spokes).

The ultimate aim must be to provide the best service and level of support for patients and their families in what is a very difficult time.

In 2007, the Mental Health Foundation found a lack of co-ordination between different mental health services for people with eating disorders—a finding echoed throughout the sector. An integrated approach through the hub-and-spoke model will directly address this issue.

Integrated Care

To work, the model needs effective formal and informal relationships between each hub and its associated spokes. This includes regular structured supervision and training combined with *ad hoc* consultation and liaison support when it is needed.

Such an approach is most effective when an individual in the spoke service has a dedicated co-ordination role, often in conjunction with a local 'virtual team' (including in some cases primary care clinicians). Team members often have a clinical interest and experience in the specialty. Closer relationships between clinicians can build closer relationships between services and a better path for patients through the varying aspects of their care.

Beyond hubs and spokes we know that within services across primary, secondary and tertiary care, multi-disciplinary teams are required to address the complexity of eating disorders treatment and associated co-morbid conditions.

This means that practitioners from medical, nursing, dietetics, psychology, psychiatry, psychotherapy and other disciplines all need to be skilled at working together. I commend ANZAED's open and multi-disciplinary approach. . . .

Clinical Leadership

It is also why clinical leadership is so important to this government. In March last year, we issued a significant document called 'In Good Hands' to help district health boards introduce greater clinical leadership into the public health system. Globally, clinical leadership is recognised as a fundamental driver of a better health service. We had heard countless stories of clinicians feeling ignored and disengaged.

As clinicians, your involvement in the further development of eating disorders services is critical. If the system is to focus on the patient we need to know what those providing care day in and day out have to say.

I am aware that at times managers and clinicians have not engaged collaboratively like we would hope. It is also worth acknowledging that there are competing visions of how best to do things and that meeting the needs of different stakeholders is sometimes challenging.

Making Services More Effective and Easier to Access

What we need is robust debate, productive engagement and partnership between funders, managers and clinicians that focuses on both fiscal discipline and clinical best practice. We also need a system that allows clinicians to be centrally involved in decisions about service configuration.

Eating disorders are complex. We all know that there are often co-morbid disorders that are present alongside eating disorders. We also know that the mortality rates for eating disorders are high. Patients and families struggle through confusing and difficult times.

It would help if services were easy for them to navigate. We have made progress to bring patient care closer to home and to provide better coverage and integration of services. But things can always be better. We need your ideas, and your input into how to make the path through treatment as smooth and effective as possible.

We also need the research evidence and clinical experience such as will be presented at this conference to inform our understanding of best practice as we deliver eating disorders services. Patients deserve nothing less. I hope you enjoy the next few days and have many thought-provoking conversations with your colleagues.

VIEWPOINT 7

The British Fashion Industry Should Show a Variety of Body Types

Fiona Bawdon

Fiona Bawdon is a journalist. In the following viewpoint, she reports that the British government is considering a range of recommendations that aim to counter the pervasive effect that images of extremely skinny models and celebrities have had on young women in the United Kingdom. One of the proposals is to warn readers when pictures of fashion models in magazines have been altered to make the models look even thinner, Bawdon explains. Another recommendation, according to the author, is to promote a more diverse mix of body types in the media and the fashion industry, sending the message that different types and sizes of bodies can be sexy and beautiful.

As you read, consider the following questions:

1. According to a Girlguiding UK study, what percentage of girls aged sixteen to twenty-five said the media made them feel that "being pretty and thin" was the "most important thing"?
2. According to a Scottish survey, how much had the rate of eating disorders increased from 1990 to 2006?

Fiona Bawdon, "No Model for Girls," *New Statesman*, September 27, 2007. www.newstatesman.com.

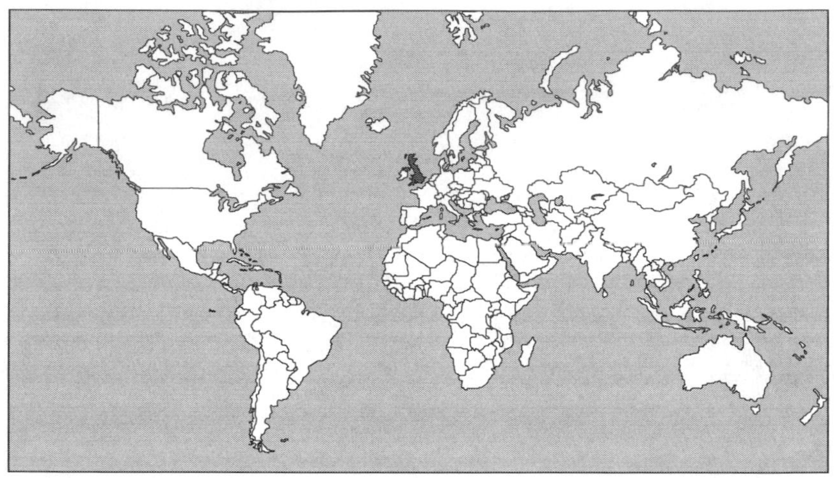

3. When asked, what is it that most eating disorders sufferers said would help prevent the condition?

There is now solid evidence that images of superthin celebrities in the media have a direct effect on the well-being of teenagers

As London Fashion Week sashayed to a close on 20 September [2007], most of the media coverage was of the clothes, rather than the skeletal frames of the girls inside them. Yet the week coincided with the publication of recommendations from a controversial inquiry into the health of fashion models, set up after two Latin American models died from eating disorders, one after collapsing on the catwalk.

The Model Health

In her report, the chair of the Model Health Inquiry, Baroness Kingsmill, said she had found "startling" evidence of the vulnerability of models, who are at "high risk" of eating disorders. The inquiry heard evidence from an editor who said she'd sat through "innumerable shows where I have been unable to take in the clothes through shock at the emaciated frames of models". A writer said the fashion world was "numb", looking at models only as "clothes hangers" and "failing to see whether they are healthy or not". The inquiry made 14 recommendations to improve the working lives of models, including banning under-16s from the catwalk and introducing compulsory medical checks and a trade union.

The importance of the report, however, is not just that it reveals exploitation of young women in the fashion industry. There is now a whole body of evidence that links fashion and media images directly to the health and well-being of the wider population of teenage girls.

Other Studies

In a study of 3,200 young women carried out in February this year by Girlguiding UK, over half of 16- to 25-year-olds said the media made them feel that "being pretty and thin" was the "most important thing". A quarter of girls aged between ten and 15 said the same. The most influential role models by far (cited by 95 per cent of girls) were Kate Moss and Victoria Beckham, both of whom are famously thin. In another study—"Sex, Drugs, Alcohol and Young People", by the Independent Advisory Group on Sexual Health and HIV, published in June this year—nearly 30 per cent of 11-year-old girls expressed dissatisfaction with their body weight, and one in ten was on a diet. By age 15, 46 per cent of girls were unhappy with their weight, and a quarter of them were dieting.

There is now a whole body of evidence that links fashion and media images directly to the health and well-being of the wider population of teenage girls.

Professionals working in this field are convinced that the number of teenage girls with an eating disorder is going up, and that sufferers are getting younger. The majority are aged 14–25, but girls as young as eight have been diagnosed. The last reliable survey into eating disorders across Britain dates back to 1990, but in Scotland, where new research was conducted in 2006, there had been a 40 per cent increase since 1990.

Teenage girls say they are influenced by pictures of impossibly skinny women, even when they don't want to be. At a recent conference in London about teenagers and the media, organised by the campaign group Women in Journalism, one teenager encapsulated the views of many of the 50 or so girls present, saying the fashion to be super-skinny made her "feel really ugly. I know it's really stupid but I still follow it. It makes me feel really insecure."

This young woman's experience is all too common, according to Professor Janet Treasure, director of the eating disorders unit at the South London and Maudsley NHS [Foundation] Trust, who has conducted research into the impact of the "size-zero culture". She says looking at pictures of thin women reduces self-esteem—and adolescents are among the most susceptible to these pressures. Adolescents are also the group most likely to suffer long-term ill effects from eating disorders because their bodies are still developing.

Addressing the Size-Zero Culture

Susan Ringwood, chief executive of Beat, the eating disorders charity, gave evidence to the inquiry. She supports its conclusions, but says restricting its remit to protecting young women in the modelling industry, rather than tackling the impact of "size-zero" culture on the wider population, was an opportunity missed.

Ringwood accepts that it's a gross oversimplification to blame the rise in eating disorders entirely on the media's focus on thinness and dieting, but says it does play a part. "Eating disorder sufferers say: 'How come it's OK for celebrities to look like that and not me? How come they're being celebrated on the front of a magazine and I'm in hospital being told I'm going to die?'"

"London Fashion Week," cartoon by Andrew Exton, www.CartoonStock.com. Copyright © Andrew Exton. Reproduction rights obtainable from www.CartoonStock.com.

Although the Model Health Inquiry acknowledged this is an area outside its remit, it included a recommendation for a code of conduct to govern the digital manipulation of photos. The inquiry heard evidence of retouching to make models look thinner or even to make ill models look well—something of great concern to those working with eating disorder sufferers. "These processes add pressure to models to meet an unattainable ideal," it said. One suggestion was for retouched photos to carry a "health warning" so that the reader knows what she's looking at isn't real. The teenagers at the London conference were previously unaware that magazine images are routinely airbrushed: thighs slimmed, wrinkles smoothed and blemishes removed.

Of course, media coverage of skinny women is far from universally positive. But even critical coverage of celebrities who are deemed to be "too thin" can make matters worse for eating disorder sufferers, according to Ringwood. Low self-esteem is a recognised factor: Sufferers don't think they are worthy of taking up any space in the world, and shrink accordingly. Seeing bodies that look similar to theirs being pilloried and described as revolting reinforces their own lack of self-worth, she says.

Bodies Beautiful

Ringwood acknowledges that the causes of eating disorders are many and complex; they include factors such as genetic disposition and personality type, often compounded by traumatic events—for instance, bereavement or bullying. "But the final piece of the jigsaw is the social context," she says. Add the media, which celebrate impossibly skinny bodies over all other types, and numbers of sufferers are bound to increase. She would welcome a move for magazines to specify when images have been retouched.

It is a view shared by many of the sufferers themselves. Asked what was the one thing that would help prevent such conditions, most sufferers said it would be for the media to show more "real" bodies. They ranked this as more important than greater understanding from parents, or even greater medical knowledge. "Why can't the media promote healthy, normal-sized people?" lamented one typical respondent.

Ringwood says the media and the fashion industry should present a more diverse mix of body types as beautiful and acceptable. Such a change would not be a total solution by any means, but it would help, she argues. "We can't change brain chemistry and we can't protect young women from all forms of trauma. Of all the factors involved in eating disorders, images in the media are the one area we can change."

Viewpoint 8

Malaysia Is Not Providing Adequate and Affordable Treatment for Eating Disorders

Ng Cheng Yee

Ng Cheng Yee is a reporter for the Star, *an English-language newspaper in Malaysia. In the following viewpoint, she asserts that although eating disorders are a rising problem in Malaysia, there are few affordable treatment options for patients. In fact, Yee asserts, there is no specialized center to treat eating disorders in the entire country. Doctors must refer patients to Singapore for treatment, which is costly and unaffordable for many suffering from the disease. According to the author, Malaysia must take steps to build a treatment center and conduct some in-depth research on the problem before it gets more serious.*

As you read, consider the following questions:

1. According to a 2005 National University of Singapore study, what percentage of female students were found to be at high risk of eating disorders?
2. How much does it cost per day for an eating disorder patient to get treatment in Singapore, according to Dr. Lai Fong Hwa?

Ng Cheng Yee, "Expert: 1 in 10 Young Girls Are Prone to Eating Disorders," *The Star, Malaysia*, June 24, 2007. thestar.com.my.

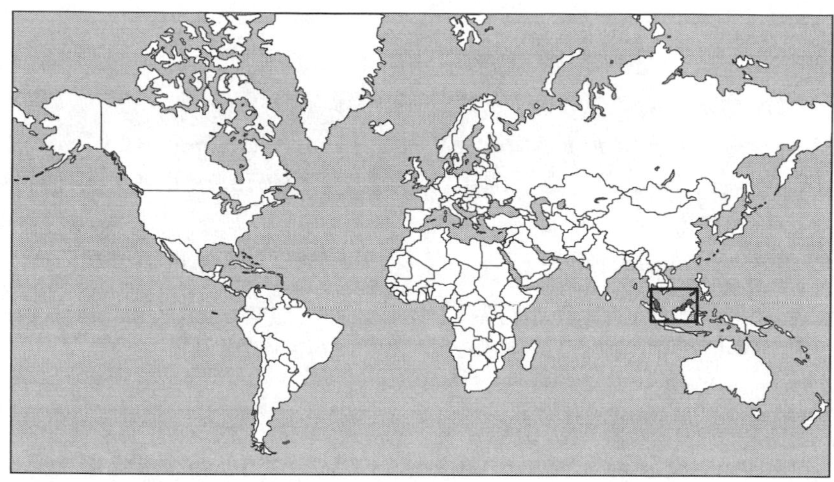

3. In what countries does the author say eating disorders are common?

Walk into any urban campus and there will be hordes of young girls who are slim and dressed in clothes that reveal their figures. Being thin is in and many are dying to be thin. They want to emulate weight-conscious celebrities like Paris Hilton and Lindsay Lohan.

The Prevalence of Eating Disorders

And this is one of the reasons for a rising problem among young females—eating disorders. About 70% of them are not satisfied with the shape—and size—of their bodies.

In a study conducted by chartered psychologist Dr Hera Lukman, it was revealed that about one in 10 young urban female college students is prone to eating disorders in their quest for a perfect body shape.

Although there are signs that this problem is on the rise, there has been no study to determine the number, as those suffering from the problem rarely seek help voluntarily.

Nevertheless, Dr Lukman said studies have shown that the prevalence of eating disorders in Asian countries was comparable to that in the West, where between 1% and 4% of girls aged between 14 and 18 have an eating disorder.

In Singapore, a National University of Singapore's (NUS) study of 4,400 female students in 2005 also showed that 7% of them were found to be at high risk of disorders like anorexia and bulimia.

Penang hospital's child and adolescent psychiatrist Dr Lai Fong Hwa said there was a sixfold increase in the incidence of eating disorders in Singapore in the last 10 years.

Distorted Self-Images

On her survey, Dr Lukman said those affected were usually terrified of gaining weight though they were underweight or emaciated.

"The students in my survey had, among others, displayed behaviour, attitude and thoughts which were associated with eating disorders. Only 28% of them were satisfied with the shape of their bodies," she said in an interview.

The dangers of eating disorders usually make headlines when a celebrity or prominent figure dies from it.

The Consequences of Eating Disorders

The two most common eating disorders are anorexia nervosa (when one engages in self-induced food restrictions and excessive exercise although underweight) and bulimia nervosa (uncontrollable overeating or bingeing, followed by self-induced vomiting and purging via the use of laxatives). The medical fraternity usually terms them as a "complex psychological problem" with "possible indirect links" with the environment.

Dr Lukman said interviews with some of the respondents revealed that they would induce vomiting after eating. Some of them would feel guilty about eating and subsequently resort to eating in isolation or "secretive eating".

Dr Lukman added that eating disorders were chronic conditions with devastating physical, psychological and social consequences when not given immediate attention and multidisciplinary approach treatment by experts like physicians, psychiatrists, dieticians and family therapists.

The dangers of eating disorders usually make headlines when a celebrity or prominent figure dies from it. In November last year [2006], Brazilian model Ana Carolina Reston, 21, was reported to have died of anorexia nervosa. She was 1.74m [metres] tall and weighed only 40kg [kilograms] when she died. Many Tinseltown celebrities like Nicole Richie and Mary-Kate Olsen are constantly under the media glare for losing weight and looking unhealthily thin.

The Cost of Treatment

On treatment for eating disorders, Dr Lukman said Malaysia has yet to have a centre for such patients and she had to refer her patients for treatment overseas, with the nearest centre in Singapore. There was dire need for such a centre to provide proper and affordable treatment for eating disorders and conduct more in-depth research on the problem.

She said patients could not seek treatment overseas due to the high costs incurred.

Dr Lai said it costs about RM1,000 a day for an eating disorder patient to get treatment in Singapore. [RM is the abbreviation for the Malaysian ringgit, the national currency.] The high cost of treatment was because of the number of professionals involved in the care.

"If Malaysia were to set up an eating disorder centre, treatment would still cost a few hundred ringgit a day, although patients who seek help at government hospitals at the moment are treated free," he said.

"The problem in Malaysia may not be as serious (compared to Singapore), but I am seeing and hearing of more such cases these days," he said.

She said it was also difficult to identify a person with eating disorders, especially Asians, because the females tend to be thinner and have a smaller frame.

Countries where eating disorders are common include Japan, South Korea, Thailand, China, Taiwan, Hong Kong, Singapore, India, Pakistan, Egypt and Israel, she added.

Dr Lukman said eating disorders are more common among females than males. For every 10 to 20 females with eating disorders, there would be one male with a similar problem.

VIEWPOINT 9

The Philippines Is Ignoring the Problem of Eating Disorders

Natasha B. Gamalinda

Natasha B. Gamalinda is a writer and editor. In the following viewpoint, she notes that the Philippine government does not keep statistics on the number of people suffering from eating disorders. This is not because there are no cases of eating disorders in the country, the author asserts; it is because such cases are considered isolated, and people do not have the money to treat family members suffering from the disease. Gamalinda reports that experts believe many cases of eating disorders go unrecognized and untreated in the Philippines.

As you read, consider the following questions:

1. What does the author list as the textbook symptoms of anorexia nervosa?
2. According to the author, what do pro-anorexia groups advocate?
3. What happened in August 2006, according to the author, that led Madrid to ban extremely thin fashion models from the Pasarela Cibeles trade fair?

Natasha B. Gamalinda, "What's ED-ing You?," *The UP Forum*, vol. 8, no. 3, May–June, 2007. www.up.edu.ph/upforum.php.

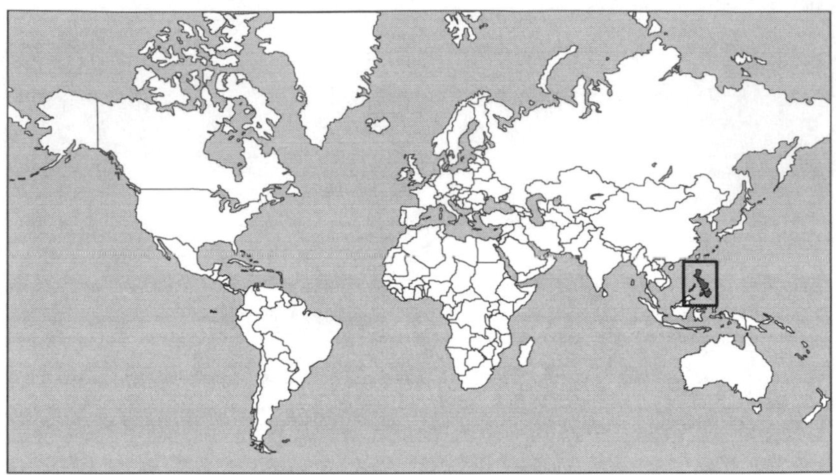

Eating disorders, like anorexia nervosa, could actually kill. Anorexia nervosa reportedly has the highest mortality rate in the USA. So why doesn't the eating disorder (ED), more popularly tagged as "Ana," make it to the statistics of the Department of Health here in the Philippines? Have we, despite globalization, developed an exceptional immunity to weight obsession?

"During wartime, people are least likely to commit suicide," says Dr. Violeta Bautista of the UP [University of the Philippines] Diliman (UPD) Department of Psychology. "So maybe it's the same thing with eating disorders and third world countries. When people are more concerned about earning enough money to be able to eat three nutritional meals a day, eating disorders are least likely to occur."

This does not mean that there are no cases of anorexia nervosa in the Philippines. But there are no statistics regarding eating disorders. Cases of anorexia nervosa or other psychological disorders having to do with body image are not accommodated in the National [Center for] Mental Health. The latter is for the treatment of other "more serious" psychological disorders, like schizophrenia or depression. "They give more attention to florid symptoms of hallucination, delusion, etc. Only severe cases of anorexia are brought in for hospitalization. These would be patients who are so thin that their state of health has been compromised. At the advanced stage, they are emaciated." Patients who have body image problems are counseled in private clinics like Dr. Bautista's. They are, also, inevitably considered "isolated" cases.

"I only had two patients here in the Philippines who came close to actually being anorexic. Both were college students. And their parents didn't think it was necessary to continue their treatments," says Dr. Bautista. "Going to the shrink is not as widely accepted in the Philippines as in the United States," she adds. Why? Well, to begin with, most people here can hardly foot the treatment's fees.

Cases of anorexia nervosa or other psychological disorders having to do with body image are not accommodated in the National [Center for] Mental Health.

What Are Eating Disorders?

Patients diagnosed with anorexia nervosa starve themselves to death because of low self-esteem. Inherently linked to a negative body image, and called the "golden girl syndrome" in the 1970s, it was believed to be a phenomenon exclusive to affluent Caucasian women. Studies in the 1990s debunked this old notion. The thin-is-beautiful ideal has spilled over the borders of the West, and has spread over Asia.

The textbook symptoms of anorexia nervosa are: dramatic weight loss in a relatively short period of time (i.e., 20% underweight); obsession with weight loss; unusual food rituals like cutting food into tiny pieces and/or chewing the food for a long time and spitting it out instead of swallowing it. Patients with anorexia are also said to suffer from amenorrhea, or loss of menstruation, for at least three months.

There are two types of anorexia nervosa—the purging and the non-purging type. The purging type usually induces vomiting, compulsively exercises, and/or abuses laxatives and diuretics to get rid of what has been eaten. The non-purging type does not exhibit these symptoms.

The term "Ana" was coined by pro-anorexia groups who aim to give anorexia nervosa a less negative connotation. Pro-ana groups advocate anorexia nervosa as a way of living, not a disorder. But it is a known fact, though, that such self-deprivation of food causes serious damage to the body.

Because anorexic patients are malnourished, they suffer from hair loss, brittle and dry skin and nails, weak bones (early osteoporosis), anemia, low blood pressure and kidney and heart failures. Among psychiatric disorders in the United States, anorexia nervosa has the highest mortality rate. It usually coexists with other psychiatric illnesses such as depression and in some cases even schizophrenia.

What Kind of Person Develops Eating Disorders?

According to Dr. Bautista, most anorexics are members of highly controlling families. The patient turns to this behavior as the only way she can control some aspect of her life. Unlike patients of its sister eating disorder "Mia" (bulimia nervosa), patients of anorexia nervosa long for command over their lives. Food restriction for anorexic patients is an expression of their individuality. Bulimics, on the other hand, succumb to loss of control which manifests in binge eating. Anorexia nervosa shares all symptoms of bulimia nervosa except for binge eating, although patients of both disorders may sometimes "swap symptoms".

There are also two types of bulimia nervosa: purging and non-purging. The purging type includes self-induced vomiting and abuse of laxatives and diuretics, while the bulimic non-purging type tries to get rid of excessive calories by compulsive exercising. The bulimic's binge-purge cycle is caused by the patient's loss of control over his/her hunger and the inevitable onset of guilt after binging. The bulimic thus tries to get rid of the evidence of his/her "sin" by purging or excessive exercise.

According to the online eating disorder guide, Something Fishy, these paradigms may change over time with more discoveries about the disorder under way. Persons suffering from any of the disorders listed in the site may or may not show all symptoms of any of the eating disorders, but it doesn't mean that they are in any less danger from the condition.

The Effect of Globalization

According to Dr. Bautista the only local full-blown case of anorexia nervosa she can recall is Snooky Serna's case, which was celebrated because she was in show business.

Bautista thinks that the situation might be similar to the situation of ADHD [attention-deficit/hyperactivity disorder] and child sexual abuse in the country. She used to get no patients suffering from these problems, "But because of globalization, because of increased openness on the subject in the media, the cases are just coming in torrents. This means that there were always closet cases of abuse, or unrecognized cases of ADHD."

Bautista adds that today eating disorders are, "being widely discussed in the print media. There's a wide market for women's magazines, and information about eating disorders is available there as well as online, in the Internet. But the issue hasn't been blown out of proportion."

Most of her Filipina patients who have body image issues are in professions which require them to be thin. Most are from the media, and all are women. She has no male patients with ED symptoms.

Modern Ideals and the Fashion Industry

An article was published online early this year [2007], reporting a sudden rise of anorexia nervosa cases in Seoul, Korea. The disorder, which affected all socioeconomic classes in the

South Asian country, is said to be brought about by the "modernized" ideals of Korea's new generation. Unlike their parents, post-war South Koreans starve themselves, not because of lack of resources due to war, but because of fashion. Korean women all over the country strive to achieve . . . model-thin bodies to fit in.

On the other side of the world, Uruguayan supermodel Luisel Ramos died last August 2006 of anorexia. Her death shook the fashion industry into realizing that their to-die-for beauty paradigm is more harmful than it seems. Ramos reached the elusive size zero that the industry aspires for—at a cost. After eating nothing but green salads and drinking Diet Coke for three months, her body gave up on her. She died of heart failure at age 22.

This led Madrid's top-level fashion show, the Pasarela Cibeles trade fair, to ban overly thin models in their program. Regional official Concha Guerra acknowledged the fact that teenagers often imitate what they see on the ramp, and this is the reason why Spain is pooling all its efforts to promote a healthier body image. Models with a body mass index (BMI) of less than 18 are banned from the show. BMI is computed by dividing your weight in kilograms by your height in meters to determine if your weight is healthy for your body structure.

According to Dr. Bautista, the idol-factor of modeling and media occurs in most of her adolescent patients. Most of them express a strong desire to be models, to be in show business, or to land a job in the performing arts—fields where apparently thin is beautiful. Dr. Bautista explains that eating disorders are especially prevalent in the media.

The Need to Conform and Belong

More than just being a "vanity" disorder, EDs are deeply ingrained in the individual's need to belong. "Among teenagers, the development of self-esteem is associated with how they look," Dr. Bautista says. "Because of the influence of the media, they define their sense of beauty based on what they hear and see on TV and in print media. A few years ago, teenagers didn't use to read a lot of magazines. Now, they're a market on their own."

In a simple setup like job applications, employers are more likely to prefer thin candidates to stout ones. "The reason behind this is the old notion that thin people are efficient and quick, while stout ones are slow or lazy.". . .

There may be no official statistics of [eating disorders] here in the Philippines yet, but weight obsession exists all right.

Bautista is quick to add that there "are also positive qualities associated with a heavier build. Stout people are believed to be funny and warm. They are generally nice to be with." But they're just not what you would envision as an executive, or an up-and-coming young professional.

There may be no official statistics of ED here in the Philippines yet, but weight obsession exists all right. Sometime in 1999, the notorious Bangkok Pills [referring to a combination drug marketed for easy weight loss] hit the Philippine market. The Bureau of Food and Drugs (BFAD) posted an advisory that all unregistered slimming capsules were a grave danger to their consumers. The public was asked to report any individual or store still selling the dreaded Bangkok Pills. It has been eight years, yet the slimming craze continues, and this, ironically, is happening alongside cases of malnutrition in the Philippines.

But even if only a minority might suffer from ED, it is a life-threatening condition and should not be ignored. As Dr. Bautista says, "my patients who are anorexic are so thin that I'm scared for them. It is a serious condition."

Periodical and Internet Sources Bibliography

The following articles have been selected to supplement the diverse views presented in this chapter.

Associated Press	"Adios! Spain Bans Skinny Mannequins in Stores," MSNBC.com, March 13, 2007. http://www.msnbc.msn.com.
Geraldine Baum	"Pushing Gauntness May Be a Crime," *Los Angeles Times*, April 17, 2008.
Doreen Carvajal	"French Legislators Approve Law Against Web Sites Encouraging Anorexia and Bulimia," *New York Times*, April 15, 2008.
Jacqueline Head	"Seeking 'Thinspiration,'" BBC News, August 8, 2007. http://news.bbc.co.uk.
John Lichfield	"France Bans Websites Promoting Anorexia 'Cult,'" *Independent* (UK), April 16, 2008.
Caroline Marcus	"Australia to Ban Ultra-Skinny Models," *Telegraph* (UK), June 27, 2010.
Karryn Miller	"OA Offers Help for People with Eating Disorders," *Japan Today*, November 29, 2008.
Judy Siegel-Itzkovich	"Medical Field Lacks Eating-Disorder Treatments," *Jerusalem Post*, November 15, 2011.
Sky News	"Anorexics Told: 'It's a Diet Gone Wrong,'" February 23, 2009. http://news.sky.com.
Allison Kaplan Sommer	"Knesset Bill Could Ban Too-Skinny Models," *Jewish Daily Forward*, June 18, 2010.
Dennis Thompson	"Eating Disorders Can Last Well Beyond Teen Years," *US News & World Report*, December 28, 2011.

For Further Discussion

Chapter 1

1. This chapter explores several conditions that have recently been classified as eating disorders or are under consideration as eating disorders. Which one do you feel is the most common? The most dangerous? The least dangerous? Support your answers with text from the viewpoints.
2. Health professionals have noted an increase in eating disorders in men and older women. Why do you think eating disorders such as anorexia nervosa are becoming more common in these groups? Explain your reasoning.

Chapter 2

1. After reading the viewpoints in this chapter, describe the connection between body image and eating disorders. What kinds of factors impact how a person feels about his or her own body? Explain.
2. How can communities deal with body image issues effectively? Offer a few suggestions on how to combat poor body image. What can you do as an individual to address the issue?

Chapter 3

1. The media are widely blamed for disseminating and promoting unhealthy and unrealistic body images that contribute to the development of eating disorders in women and men. How much responsibility do the media have in this regard? Explicate your position on the media's role.

2. What steps can the media take to combat eating disorders? Suggest a few things the media can do to address body image and eating disorders, and explain how they can make a difference.

Chapter 4

1. A number of strategies to fight eating disorders are discussed in this chapter. Which do you think has the most potential? Which do you think will be the least effective? Why?

Organizations to Contact

The editors have compiled the following list of organizations concerned with the issues debated in this book. The descriptions are derived from materials provided by the organizations. All have publications or information available for interested readers. The list was compiled on the date of publication of the present volume; the information provided here may change. Be aware that many organizations take several weeks or longer to respond to inquiries, so allow as much time as possible.

American Medical Association (AMA)
515 N. State Street, Chicago, IL 60654
(800) 621-8335
website: www.ama-assn.org

The American Medical Association (AMA) was established in 1847 to improve the state of the American health system and the health of Americans. The AMA brings health professionals together to formulate more effective strategies to treat eating disorders, disordered eating, and malnutrition. The association works to allocate resources, research, and treatment for the growing epidemic of eating disorders and provides fact sheets and studies for health care professionals who deal with the weight-related disease. The AMA publishes the *Journal of the American Medical Association*, a world-renowned periodical that researches health issues and treatments, and the *AMA Wire*, a weekly e-newsletter that features breaking medical news and information on topics of interest.

Binge Eating Disorder Association (BEDA)
637 Emerson Place, Severna Park, MD 21146
(855) 855-2332 • fax: (410) 741-3037
e-mail: info@bedaonline.com
website: www.bedaonline.com

The Binge Eating Disorder Association (BEDA) is an American organization that is "committed to facilitating awareness, excellence in care, and recovery for those who live and those who work with binge eating disorder through outreach and support, education, and resources." BEDA is dedicated to improving prevention, diagnosis, and treatment for binge eating disorder. It also offers resources on its website, including links to other organizations, breaking news, updates on recent programs, and a calendar of events. BEDA also disseminates information on binge eating and its effects on the individual, the family, and the community.

Eating Disorders Coalition (EDC)
720 Seventh Street NW, Ste. 300, Washington, DC 20001
(202) 543-9570
e-mail: manager@eatingdisorderscoalition.org
website: www.eatingdisorderscoalition.org

The Eating Disorders Coalition (EDC) is an advocacy organization that was formed to ensure that the US government recognizes and prioritizes eating disorders as a public health problem and invests in research, education, and treatment options. EDC raises awareness of eating disorders among policy makers and the public and lobbies for policies that prevent eating disorders and support the healthy development of children. Another mission of the EDC is to mobilize and empower individuals and families for increased funding, better awareness and education, and effective programs and policies to prevent, diagnose, and treat eating disorders. The EDC website features updates on legislative efforts, upcoming events, and breaking news.

Middle East Eating Disorders Association (MEEDA)
e-mail: jalford@themeeda.com
website: www.themeeda.com

Founded in 2009, the Middle East Eating Disorders Association (MEEDA) is a nonprofit organization that was established to raise awareness about eating disorders and provide resources to individuals and families affected by anorexia nervosa, bulimia, and related disorders. The organization's mission statement is, "Being active in the community; providing workshops; organizing local, regional and international conferences and encouraging further research in the field to help identify the prevalence rate of eating disorders and help improve the quality of care, while working closely with physicians and other healthcare professionals is at the heart of what MEEDA stands for." The MEEDA website features links to video documentaries, research, and fact sheets about eating disorders.

National Association of Anorexia Nervosa and Associated Disorders (ANAD)
PO Box 640, Naperville, IL 60566
(630) 577-1333
e-mail: anadhelp@anad.org
website: www.anad.org

The National Association of Anorexia Nervosa and Associated Disorders (ANAD) is a nonprofit organization that works to combat the serious problem of eating disorders, especially anorexia nervosa and bulimia. ANAD describes its mission as promoting eating disorders awareness; encouraging better prevention and diagnosis; and supporting individuals, families, and medical professionals. ANAD hosts an annual conference to bring together health professionals, researchers and scientists, and experts in the field to exchange information and learn about new technology, programs, and therapies. ANAD also has a range of information and resources available on its website, including its quarterly newsletter.

National Centre for Eating Disorders (NCFED)
54 New Road, Esher, Surrey K10 9NU
England
0845 838 2040 • fax: 01372 469550
website: www.eating-disorders.org.uk

The National Centre for Eating Disorders (NCFED) was founded in 1984 to provide resources and treatment for women and men afflicted with eating disorders in the United

Kingdom. NCFED trains health professionals working with eating disorders and offers personal, phone, e-mail, and group therapy. It also offers support to families and friends of those battling eating disorders. There is a plethora of information available on the group's website, including a bookstore and resource library.

National Eating Disorders Association (NEDA)
165 W. Forty-Sixth Street, New York, NY 10036
(212) 575-6200 • fax: (212) 575-1650
e-mail: info@NationalEatingDisorders.org
website: www.nationaleatingdisorders.org

The National Eating Disorders Association (NEDA) is a nonprofit organization dedicated to advocating for men and women suffering from eating disorders and their families; providing the most recent information on therapies and treatments for eating disorders; and ensuring access to the most up-to-date and effective resources for families and medical professionals dealing with these diseases. NEDA campaigns for prevention of eating disorders and better funding for research and treatment. It also raises awareness of eating disorders and the resources available to individuals and families through a variety of activities and programs, including the National Eating Disorders Awareness Week and NEDA walks, as well as lectures, seminars, and an annual conference. The NEDA website features a range of information and resources, including stories from men and women recovering from eating disorders and stories from their families.

National Eating Disorder Information Centre (NEDIC)
ES 7-421, 200 Elizabeth Street
Toronto, Ontario M5G 2C4
Canada
(416) 340-4156 • fax: (416) 340-4736
e-mail: nedic@uhn.ca
website: www.nedic.ca

The National Eating Disorder Information Centre (NEDIC) is a nonprofit organization that offers information and resources to individuals and families on eating disorders and related issues. NEDIC identifies its mission as educational, and it works to raise awareness of eating disorders among policy makers and the public. NEDIC staffs a national hotline for men and women who suffer from disordered eating; coordinates workshops for communities to inform citizens about eating disorders and treatment; and sets up public awareness campaigns such as Eating Disorder Awareness Week in Canada. The NEDIC website has a resource library, which includes links to websites, articles, videos, personal stories, and periodicals.

Renfrew Center Foundation
475 Spring Lane, Philadelphia, PA 19128
(877) 367-3383 • fax: (215) 482-2695
e-mail: info@renfrew.org
website: www.renfrew.org

The Renfrew Center Foundation was established in 1990 to raise awareness among the public and professionals about the dangers of anorexia nervosa, bulimia, and other eating disorders. The organization works to train professionals to recognize and effectively treat such disorders; funds and coordinates research; and lobbies legislators and policy makers to remove barriers to new therapies and treatment. The Renfrew Center Foundation website features information on upcoming events and programs, educational and training materials, links to community resources, and research on eating disorders in the United States.

Royal Society of Medicine
1 Wimpole Street, London W1G 0AE
England
(+44) (0) 20 7290 2900
website: www.rsm.ac.uk

The Royal Society of Medicine is the largest provider of medical education in the United Kingdom. The independent association has developed a range of educational programs and activities meant to keep health care professionals updated on the latest research, treatment programs, and medical information available. It also offers a forum for doctors, nurses, dentists, and other health professionals to exchange ideas and techniques. The Royal Society of Medicine publishes the *Journal of the Royal Society of Medicine*, a monthly periodical that covers the latest research and in-depth articles on medical topics, including rising rates of eating disorders in England, Wales, and Scotland.

World Health Organization (WHO)
Avenue Appia 20, Geneva 27 1211
Switzerland
(+41) 22 791 21 11 • fax: (+41) 22 791 31 11
e-mail: info@who.int
website: www.who.int

The World Health Organization (WHO) is the United Nations agency responsible for directing global health care matters. WHO funds research on issues that affect global health, including the spreading problem of eating disorders and weight-related diseases. The agency monitors health trends, compiles useful statistics, and offers technical support to countries dealing with the consequences of eating disorders. The WHO website features podcasts, blogs, and video; it also offers fact sheets, reports, studies, and a calendar of events. There are a broad range of articles on the website, including those dealing with nutrition-related topics such as malnutrition and eating disorders.

Bibliography of Books

Nancy Alcorn	*Beyond Starved: Mercy for Eating Disorders: Real Stories of Real Freedom with Bonus Study Guide.* Enumclaw, WA: WinePress, 2009.
June Alexander and Janet Treasure, eds.	*A Collaborative Approach to Eating Disorders.* London: Routledge, 2012.
Jane Bingham	*Eating Disorders.* Pleasantville, NY: Gareth Stevens Publishing, 2009.
Harriet Brown	*Brave Girl Eating: A Family's Struggle with Anorexia.* New York: William Morrow, 2010.
Steven Gerali	*What Do I Do When Teenagers Struggle with Eating Disorders?* Grand Rapids, MI: Zondervan, 2010.
Simona Giordano	*Exercise and Eating Disorders: An Ethical and Legal Analysis.* New York: Routledge, 2010.
Simon G. Gowers and Lynne Green	*Eating Disorders: Cognitive Behaviour Therapy with Children and Young People.* New York: Routledge, 2009.
Meredith Seafield Grant	*Road to the Rainbow: A Personal Journey to Recovery from an Eating Disorder Survivor.* 2nd ed. Terrace, British Columbia: CCB Publishing, 2008.

Trisha Gura — *Lying in Weight: The Hidden Epidemic of Eating Disorders in Adult Women*. New York: HarperCollins, 2007.

Nicole Johns — *Purge: Rehab Diaries*. Berkeley, CA: Seal Press, 2009.

Bryan Lask and Ian Frampton, eds. — *Eating Disorders and the Brain*. Chichester, West Sussex, England: John Wiley & Sons, 2011.

Yael Latzer, Joav Merrick, and Daniel Stein, eds. — *Understanding Eating Disorders: Integrating Culture, Psychology and Biology*. New York: Nova Science, 2011.

Daniel Le Grange and James Locke, eds. — *Eating Disorders in Children and Adolescents: A Clinical Handbook*. New York: Guilford Press, 2011.

Aimee Liu — *Gaining: The Truth About Life After Eating Disorders*. New York: Warner Books, 2007.

Helen Malson and Maree Burns, eds. — *Critical Feminist Approaches to Eating Disorders*. New York: Routledge, 2009.

Courtney E. Martin — *Perfect Girls, Starving Daughters: How the Quest for Perfection Is Harming Young Women*. New York: Berkley Books, 2008.

Johanna Marie McShane and Tony Paulson — *Why She Feels Fat: Understanding Your Loved One's Eating Disorder and How You Can Help*. Carlsbad, CA: Gurze Books, 2008.

Kate Middleton	*Eating Disorders: The Path to Recovery*. Oxford, England: Lion, 2007.
Abigail Horvitz Natenshon	*Doing What Works: An Integrative System for the Treatment of Eating Disorders from Diagnosis to Recovery*. Washington, DC: NASW Press/ National Association of Social Workers, 2009.
Jane Ogden	*The Psychology of Eating: From Healthy to Disordered Behavior*. 2nd ed. Malden, MA: Wiley-Blackwell, 2010.
Jenni Schaefer	*Goodbye ED, Hello Me: Recover from Your Eating Disorder and Fall in Love with Life*. New York: McGraw-Hill, 2009.
Michele Siegel, Judith Brisman, and Margot Weinshel	*Surviving an Eating Disorder: Strategies for Families and Friends*. 3rd ed. New York: Collins Living, 2009.
Ron A. Thompson and Roberta Trattner Sherman	*Eating Disorders in Sport*. New York: Brunner-Routledge, 2010.
Edward T. Welch	*Eating Disorders: The Quest for Thinness*. Greensboro, NC: New Growth Press, 2008.

Index

Geographic headings and page numbers in **boldface** refer to viewpoints about that country or region.

A

F

G

H

N

O

P

R

S

T

07 13